Martin Cox has been teaching for 25
in primary schools, has now moved
in Music, Drama and RE. He remains convinced that collective worship is a golden opportunity to reflect on important concepts such as what Christians believe and what they have to celebrate. Friends help to field-test his assemblies and suggest changes. He is happy for people to take his ideas and use them as a springboard for their own creativity.

In his spare time, Martin likes to compose for choirs. He acts as musical director and accompanist to two theatre groups and occasionally steps out from behind the keyboard to perform in the chorus. He is just as happy helping others to show off their skills as being on the stage. He loves to work on songs from the shows and has a regular slot helping with pantomimes. When he sits down, he's usually either eating or reading crime fiction.

Martin lives in Beverley, East Yorkshire, and has three teenage children.

Text copyright © Martin Cox 2010
The author asserts the moral right
to be identified as the author of this work

Published by
The Bible Reading Fellowship
15 The Chambers, Vineyard
Abingdon OX14 3FE
United Kingdom
Tel: +44 (0)1865 319700
Email: enquiries@brf.org.uk
Website: www.brf.org.uk
BRF is a Registered Charity

ISBN 978 1 84101 701 3

First published 2010
10 9 8 7 6 5 4 3 2 1 0
All rights reserved

Acknowledgments
Unless otherwise stated, scripture quotations are taken from the Contemporary English
Version of the Bible published by HarperCollins Publishers, copyright © 1991, 1992, 1995
American Bible Society.

A catalogue record for this book is available from the British Library

Printed in Singapore by Craft Print International Ltd

Assemblies

for Spring and Summer Festivals

36 ready-to-use ideas for key Christian festivals
and other special days

Martin Cox

To my mother, Win, for her love and advice over many years.

Acknowledgments

I am very grateful once again to all at BRF for their advice and help while I have been preparing the book for publication, especially Sue Doggett, Commissioning Editor for Barnabas books.

Important information

Photocopying permission

The Copyright Licensing Agency (CLA)

Contents

Part One: Assemblies for spring and summer festivals

January

February

March

Part Two: Ideas for cross-curricular work

Part Three: Appendices

Foreword

This book is a worthy successor to the excellent *Assemblies for Autumn Festivals* by Martin Cox. Martin has skilfully avoided the pitfalls and superficial tokenism that a book on festivals can fall into and has yet again produced an enticing array of Christian festivals and significant days that should whet the appetite of anyone planning collective worship.

There is a winning combination of educational content and worship opportunities and, as before, the Appendix contains ideas for cross-curricular links that would support the development of the creative curriculum and stimulate interesting classroom discussions and projects.

The format is straightforward: there is a Bible story, information for the teacher, and then some inviting ideas for exploring the theme, followed by suggestions for songs or hymns and a simple prayer.

A good test of any book of ideas for collective worship is to see whether they have dared to tackle that trickiest of celebrations, Trinity—and Martin does not disappoint. He has tackled the concept using Design Technology, Literacy and Maths while introducing the reader to the idea that some subjects are so mysterious and complex that even a lifetime of study might not plumb their depths and intricacies.

One of my greatest pleasures as a teacher was leading assemblies and collective worship, and I only wish that this book had been available to me. I am certain that it will prove itself to be an invaluable asset for anyone planning school assemblies and collective worship.

Elizabeth Wolverson
Director, School Support Services, London Diocesan Board for Schools

⊕

Introduction

This book is a companion volume to *Assemblies for Autumn Festivals* (Barnabas, 2007). It is in the same format to enable you to use it in a flexible way to lead collective worship. You can dip in and use any assembly that suits your needs, but there are two fuller approaches that will both work well.

Date order

First of all, you might use the assemblies in the order in which they are set out. The Contents page shows the month in which each assembly might be suitable, and exact festival dates are given, where appropriate, at the beginning of each assembly. For many seasonal assemblies, such as Easter, the date will be different each year. These seasonal assemblies are listed under the month in which they most often fall.

Some months offer more assemblies than others, depending on the number of festivals or celebration days that fall in those months.

Key themes

Alternatively, you could choose one of the four themes from the grid on page 12. The themes are expanded in Part Two, with further links to the curriculum (see pages 180–191). See also Appendix 1 (pages 202–204).

Whatever approach you choose, please take a few moments to read through the key background information for each assembly and then decide which of the resources you might choose to use. Sometimes the resources are essential and at other times optional; sometimes a choice is needed. Some of the assemblies are more interactive, others more visual. Different ideas may work better in your context, and you'll know what to use. So much material can now be accessed via the Internet, by using search engines such as www.google.com or www.yahoo.com, that illustration templates have not been included. Particular images have sometimes been suggested, however, as have related websites.

Bible references

Bible references are given to support the stories. The key passage is often the Bible story, which is followed by further relevant links. These can be used within the assembly as appropriate, or in classroom follow-up work.

Suggestions for songs

Appropriate songs are suggested to accompany each assembly. It is expected that most schools will have a copy of the BBC book *Come and Praise*. Other useful song books include *Junior Praise*, *Kidsource*, *Our Singing School*, *The Rainbow Songbook* and *The Source*. In addition, you will find suggested songs from the 'Out of the Ark' *Songs for Every…* series with their super CD backing tracks. There is also a *Words on Screen* package for use with interactive whiteboards. (These seem to work with the newest IT equipment most commonly found in schools.) When looking for famous hymns, any traditional hymn book will come in handy, such as *Hymns Old and New*. It is always good to use a mixture of traditional and modern hymns during a term, choosing the best of the old and the new. See pages 205–211 for an index of songs.

CDs can also be used as an alternative to live music, including the excellent set by Kevin Mayhew Music.

Suggested songs are listed with their song book numbers. Abbreviations are as follows:

CP: Come and Praise
HON: Hymns Old and New
JP: Junior Praise
KS: Kidsource
OSS: Our Singing School
RS: The Rainbow Songbook
TS: The Source

Ideas for cross-curricular work

Part Two includes further background information on all four themes, along with a selection of ideas for unpacking the themes in the classroom. Many of these suggestions could be used within lesson time linked to work in RE, Art, Citizenship and Literacy as well as other curriculum subjects.

The ideas in the key themes sometimes overlap. For example, any discussion of the famous saints of Britain easily leads on to thoughts about how people in more recent times have lived out their beliefs, showing their faith in action. The life of Jesus naturally influences much of the structure of the Christian year but, of course, the theme of 'celebrations' will expand further as children mark birthdays and other family occasions among their special days.

The chapter on the life of Jesus includes follow-up ideas for Easter and the ascension, but ideas for Pentecost appear in the 'Special days and celebrations' chapter. You are encouraged to look across the themes to find all the ideas that might be useful on a given occasion.

Ways to use the assemblies

Grid of themes

SAINTS OF BRITAIN	FAITH IN ACTION	THE LIFE OF JESUS	SPECIAL DAYS AND CELEBRATIONS
David	*Bible disciples:*	Epiphany	Shrove Tuesday
Patrick	Paul	Baptism	Ash Wednesday
George	Mark	Candlemas	Lent 1
Bede	Barnabas	Lent 2	Mothering Sunday
Boniface	Peter 1	Annunciation	Pentecost
Richard	Peter 2	Palm Sunday	Trinity
Alban	Thomas	Easter	Fathers' Day
Swithun	*Later disciples:*	Ascension	Sea Sunday
	Martin Luther King		Leavers' service
	Gladys Aylward		
	George Müller		
	Florence Nightingale		
	John and Charles Wesley		

Part One

Assemblies for spring and summer festivals

⊕

Good news for everyone

Date: 6 January
Theme: The life of Jesus
Curriculum links: Geography, RE

Quite often, in order to complete the Christmas narrative, we include the visit of the wise men in our nativity plays. There is a great deal of sense in this as it makes a key point that the message of Jesus' coming was not just for the Jewish nation but for the whole world.

The word 'Epiphany' means 'showing' or 'revealing'. Christians believe that we know about God because he shows aspects of his nature to us. The biblical story of salvation is rather like a jigsaw puzzle, with more and more pieces falling progressively into place. God's plan is all-embracing: he wants to be known throughout the whole of the world that he made. However, for Christians, nothing in the story makes full sense without Jesus.

Bible story

When Jesus was born in the village of Bethlehem in Judea, Herod was king. During this time some wise men from the east came to Jerusalem and said, 'Where is the child born to be king of the Jews? We saw his star in the east and have come to worship him.'

When King Herod heard about this, he was worried, and so was everyone else in Jerusalem. Herod brought together the chief priests and the teachers of the Law of Moses and asked them, 'Where will the Messiah be born?'

They told him, 'He will be born in Bethlehem, just as the prophet wrote, "Bethlehem in the land of Judea, you are very important among the towns of Judea. From your town will come a leader, who will be like a shepherd for my people Israel."'

Herod secretly called in the wise men and asked them when they had first seen the star. He told them, 'Go to Bethlehem and search carefully for the child. As soon as you find him, let me know. I want to go and worship him too.'

The wise men listened to what the king said and then left. And the star they had seen in the east went on ahead of them until it stopped over the place where the child was. They were thrilled and excited to see the star.

When the men went into the house and saw the child with Mary, his mother, they knelt down and worshipped him. They took out their gifts of gold, frankincense, and myrrh and gave them to him. Later they were warned in a dream not to return to Herod, and they went back home by another road.

MATTHEW 2:1–12

Bible links

Ask, and you will receive. Search, and you will find. Knock, and the door will be opened for you. Everyone who asks will receive. Everyone who searches will find. And the door will be opened for everyone who knocks.

MATTHEW 7:7–8

God loved the people of this world so much that he gave his only Son, so that everyone who has faith in him will have eternal life and never really die.

JOHN 3:16

Key background information for the teacher

God's plan has been developing down the centuries, starting with Abraham and his family and on to the nation of people he established until, through Jesus and his followers, God reached out to the whole world. Matthew recorded the story of the wise men to show not only that Jesus' birth fulfilled the ancient scriptures but also that it was significant for more than just people of Jewish faith. Christians believe that whatever our language, race or country of origin, God's welcome into his family is for every person in every nation.

Suggestions for visual aids and resources

- A globe
- A Christmas card showing the wise men travelling to Bethlehem or at the stable, or a reproduction of a famous painting
- Four giant jigsaw pieces made from card (or four pieces of A4 card), showing the following words:
  - ❖ *(On the front)* Abraham: a very special family; *(on the back)* God's plan…
  - ❖ *(On the front)* The people of Israel: a very special nation; *(on the back)* to show
  - ❖ *(On the front)* Jesus: a very special person; *(on the back)* his love for
  - ❖ *(On the front)* The Church: a very special people; *(on the back)* the whole world

Ideas for exploring the theme

(Hold up the globe.) Say: If you wanted to get a message to everyone, how would you do it? Use a satellite, send an email, get the president of the USA to announce it…? Christians believe that God chose an even more unusual method—he sent his Son, Jesus.

God's plan to show himself to the world was rather like a giant jigsaw puzzle being completed over many years. *(Have the four cards or jigsaw pieces ready to reveal as follows.)*

Piece one: Way back in history, God chose a man called Abraham and promised him that his family would be very special. They would be the ancestors of a great nation of people.

Piece two: The special nation that grew out of Abraham's family was not always good at listening to God, and yet God kept repeating his promise to look after them. He also said that he would bless the whole world through them. This was one of the reasons they were special—they weren't to keep their knowledge of God to themselves but to share it as a blessing for everyone.

But God's people lost their way and, although God didn't stop loving them, their love for him was sometimes hard to see. It got muddled up with lots of laws and duties. People who really loved God tried to draw his people back to obey and serve him. God promised to send someone special to help—someone who would be born in Bethlehem and would be a Saviour for the world. Who could this special person be? The clues were spotted by some wise men from the east who studied the ancient writings and were led to Bethlehem to see God's newborn king for themselves. (Show Christmas card or image of the wise men.)

Piece three: Christians believe that Jesus came to show everyone what God is like. He taught everyone what was at the heart of all the laws and ways of worship that had been given as a pattern so many centuries before. But, above all, he came to bring people back into a relationship with God.

Piece four: Christians everywhere have tried to follow Jesus' example, to teach about God's love and to make the world a better place.

(Turn the cards over and let the children put them together to reveal the words 'God's plan… to show his love for the whole world'.) Christians believe that God welcomes everyone into his family. Jesus' message of love is not just good news for the Church; it's good news for everyone. The Bible reminds us that everyone searching for more of God finds him, just like the wise men who came looking for Jesus all those years ago.

Suggestions for songs

- Seek ye first the kingdom of God (HON 442)
- We three kings (HON 537)
- As with gladness men of old (HON 41)
- He's got the whole world (CP 19)

Suggested prayer

Dear God, help us to be like the wise men who wanted to know more about you and went searching to find out more. Help us to remember how much you love each one of us and how you sent Jesus to show us what you are like. Help us to learn more and more from all he did and said. Amen

⊕

— Baptism of Christ —

This is my Son

Date: First Sunday after Epiphany
Theme: The life of Jesus
Curriculum links: PSHE, RE

This assembly focuses on the baptism of Jesus as the point when he
was revealed as God's Son. It was the beginning of the time when
Jesus started to teach about God, heal people who were unwell and
train his disciples. His identity was revealed and a dove appeared as
a sign of the Holy Spirit. All three members of the Trinity are evident
in this story.

Bible story

Years later, John the Baptist started preaching in the desert of
Judea. He said, 'Turn back to God! The kingdom of heaven will
soon be here.' John was the one the prophet Isaiah was talking
about, when he said, 'In the desert someone is shouting, "Get
the road ready for the Lord! Make a straight path for him."' …

'I baptise you with water so that you will give up your sins.
But someone more powerful is going to come, and I am not
good enough even to carry his sandals. He will baptise you with
the Holy Spirit and with fire…'

Jesus left Galilee and went to the Jordan River to be baptised
by John. But John kept objecting and said, 'I ought to be
baptised by you. Why have you come to me?' Jesus answered,
'For now this is how it should be, because we must do all that
God wants us to do.' Then John agreed. So Jesus was baptised.

And as soon as he came out of the water, the sky opened, and he saw the Spirit of God coming down on him like a dove. Then a voice from heaven said, 'This is my own dear Son, and I am pleased with him.'

MATTHEW 3:1–3, 11, 13–17

Bible link

You have looked deep into my heart, Lord, and you know all about me.

PSALM 139:1

Key background information for the teacher

John the Baptist was Jesus' cousin. His father, Zechariah, was told that John would be a prophet who would prepare the way for Jesus. Before Jesus started his public ministry, John went into the Judean desert to tell people to turn back to God. He used the waters of the River Jordan to show that people's sins were forgiven. John said that Jesus would cleanse people with the Holy Spirit rather than water.

There is much debate about why Jesus, as the Son of God, should need to be baptised for the forgiveness of sins. Various suggestions have been made—for example, that Jesus' baptism validated John's ministry; that it gave God an opportunity to speak in a dramatic situation; that it prepared Jesus for his time in the desert, straight afterwards, battling with temptations from the devil; or that it was a symbolic demonstration that it was time to start the job he had been sent to do.

Jesus' baptism is celebrated in the Christian calendar on the Sunday immediately after the Epiphany, which marks the time when the wise men revealed who they thought Jesus was from their study of the stars. Some 30 years later, Jesus is about to begin what he was born to do—sharing with the world the good news of God's love. The dove, a symbol of the Holy Spirit, alights on Jesus as he rises from the water.

Suggestions for visual aids and resources

- A driving licence, birth certificate and passport
- A picture or outline shape of a dove

Ideas for exploring the theme

Say: Have you ever been in a bad mood? What caused you to be so upset? What about when you are in a good mood? What causes you to be so happy? The Bible shows us that God, too, can be upset or full of joy and happiness. In our Bible story today, God shows how pleased he is with Jesus—his own dear Son.

I wonder if you can think of any ways in which we can prove who we are. Everyone is given a birth certificate when they are born. Later on, we might have a passport or a driving licence. (*Show these items to the children.*) People knew that Jesus was the son of Joseph and Mary and that he was a carpenter from Nazareth, but God chose the moment when Jesus came to be baptised by his cousin John to show everyone that he was much more than that. As Jesus came up from under the water, a dove gently landed on him and a voice was heard to say, 'This is my own dear Son, and I am pleased with him.'

God was very happy. Hundreds of years before, God had promised to send a special servant to do his work; and here was Jesus, about to start that work. God identified his Son through his words and through the dove that gently rested on him. (*Show picture or outline shape of a dove.*) Jesus was being reminded of who he was and what he was being asked to do. Everyone present was left in no doubt that Jesus was special to God. He was God's Son and everyone needed to listen to his message.

Suggestions for songs

- Spirit of God (CP 63)
- Take my life (HON 464)
- When Jesus walked in Galilee (CP 25)

Suggested prayer

Dear God, thank you for sending Jesus to show us more of what you are like. Thank you that you send your Holy Spirit to help those who believe that Jesus is your Son and want to follow his teaching. Amen

⊕

— Martin Luther King —

Peacemaker

Date: Third Monday in January (US national holiday in his honour)
Alternative date: 4 April (date of his assassination)
Theme: Faith in action (later disciples)
Curriculum links: History, PSHE

This assembly focuses on the important role of peacemaker, using the life of Martin Luther King as an example but applying it to the school playground.

Bible story

God blesses those people who are humble. The earth will belong to them! God blesses those people who want to obey him more than to eat or drink. They will be given what they want! God blesses those people who are merciful. They will be treated with mercy! God blesses those people whose hearts are pure. They will see him! God blesses those people who make peace. They will be called his children! God blesses those people who are treated badly for doing right. They belong to the kingdom of heaven.

God will bless you when people insult you, ill-treat you, and tell all kinds of evil lies about you because of me. Be happy and excited! You will have a great reward in heaven. People did these same things to the prophets who lived long ago.

MATTHEW 5:5–12

Bible links

Each of you is now a new person. You are becoming more and more like your Creator, and you will understand him better. It doesn't matter if you are a Greek or a Jew… you may be a slave or a free person. Yet Christ is all that matters, and he lives in all of us. God loves you and has chosen you as his own special people. So be gentle, kind, humble, meek, and patient.

COLOSSIANS 3:10–12

And when you were baptised, it was as though you had put on Christ in the same way you put on new clothes. Faith in Christ Jesus is what makes each of you equal with each other, whether you are a Jew or a Greek, a slave or a free person, a man or a woman. So if you belong to Christ, you are now part of Abraham's family, and you will be given what God has promised.

GALATIANS 3:27–29

Key background information for the teacher

Slavery was abolished in the UK over 200 years ago but it took longer to ensure it was truly eradicated. Even today, it could be argued that the rights of ethnic minorities, although established in law, are not always upheld. This was also the case in the USA, which abolished slavery after Britain. In the period after the Second World War, black people didn't have the same rights as white people. For example, they could not use the same restaurants, and if a white person got on to a crowded bus, a black person would have to give up his or her seat.

This made black people angry, and a young Baptist minister called Martin Luther King could see that the situation was getting more serious: it was leading to fights. He spent time praying, asking God what he should do. He knew in his heart that what was happening to black people was against God's wishes, and he decided to speak out against it, encouraging a form of non-violent protest. People listened to his advice and, even though there were huge demonstrations and marches, they never became violent. Because of what he said, and because of the way the people put their view across without causing bloodshed, many white people saw sense and supported a change in the law.

Martin Luther King is well known for his work on racial abuse but also spoke strongly against poverty and against war on behalf of people of every race. His most famous speech is probably the one in which he spoke about his vision that everyone, whatever their colour, should live together in peace. This, he believed, was what God wanted: it fulfilled the idea of God's promised land.

Martin Luther King rooted his words in both the constitution of the USA and the Bible. His speech is readily available on the Internet and recordings can be found on websites such as www.youtube.com. The total duration of the speech is approximately 17 minutes, but there are several key phrases that could be chosen to illustrate the content:

'I have a dream that one day ... the sons of former slaves and the sons of former slave owners will be able to sit down together at the table of brotherhood.'

'I have a dream that my four little children will one day live in a nation where they will not be judged by the colour of their skin but by the content of their character.'

'I have a dream today.'

'I have a dream that one day... little black boys and black girls will be able to join hands with little white boys and white girls as sisters and brothers.'

'Let freedom ring.'

'And when this happens... we will be able to speed up that day when all of God's children... will be able to join hands and sing... "Free at last, free at last. Thank God Almighty, we are free at last."'

Martin Luther King was awarded the Nobel Peace Prize in 1964 but not everyone agreed with his views. He was assassinated four years later, on 4 April 1968.

Suggestions for visual aids and resources

- The words 'I have a dream...' on a card or in a speech bubble
- The words 'God blesses those people who make peace. They will be called his children!' on a card or in a speech bubble

Ideas for exploring the theme

Begin with a short prepared role-play of a playground incident in which someone comes along to help sort out an argument, acting as a peacemaker. Alternatively, ask the children to give an example of an argument they have witnessed or taken part in on the playground.

Sometimes whole groups of people get into arguments. It can be very difficult to get them to understand each other's views. Sometimes people are treated differently because of where they come from, how they speak, what they look like, and so on. The Bible makes it very clear that this is not what God wants. It also recognises that arguments will happen and that special people are needed who will act as peacemakers. Jesus said that peacemakers will be blessed by God and will be called his children. Christians believe that it is the job of Jesus' followers to be peaceful and to be peacemakers. God also wants people to be treated fairly. Sometimes Christians have to work hard to persuade people in authority to change unjust laws.

Explain Martin Luther King's situation during the 1960s.

Share the key background information, according to the age and understanding of the children. Conclude by saying how important changes were brought about because one person sensed that God wanted him to be a peacemaker. Martin Luther King looked around and saw things that were wrong. He asked God what he should do about it and he read his Bible to look for advice. Then he chose a path of action that he thought fitted in with the way Jesus would have acted. He studied hard and didn't give up on what he knew to be right. Today, American people have a special holiday each year to remember him.

Suggestions for songs

• Peace is flowing like a river (HON 412)

Suggested prayers

Thank you, God, for the inspiring life of Martin Luther King. Thank you that he looked to you and your words for advice. Thank you that you value peacemakers so highly. Help us to remember that each person is special and unique. Amen

Disturb us, Lord, when we are too pleased with ourselves; when our dreams have come true because we dreamed too little; when we arrived safely because we sailed too close to the shore. Amen
FRANCIS DRAKE

⊕

Strike a light!

Date: 25 January
Theme: Faith in action (Bible disciples)
Curriculum links: Drama, RE

Occasionally, we hear stories in the media about how people's lives are turned upside-down by tragedy or success, sometimes even by a religious experience. In the Bible, Saul had an experience like this as he travelled to Damascus to arrest the people who followed Jesus. His encounter with Jesus changed his life to the extent that he became one of the most ardent supporters of Christianity. His transformation reminds us that, according to Christian belief, knowing Jesus as a personal friend can change people's lives.

Bible story

Saul kept on threatening to kill the Lord's followers. He even went to the high priest and asked for letters to the Jewish leaders in Damascus. He did this because he wanted to arrest and take to Jerusalem any man or woman who had accepted the Lord's Way. When Saul had almost reached Damascus, a bright light from heaven suddenly flashed around him. He fell to the ground and heard a voice that said, 'Saul! Saul! Why are you so cruel to me?'

'Who are you?' Saul asked. 'I am Jesus,' the Lord answered. 'I am the one you are so cruel to. Now get up and go into the city, where you will be told what to do.'

The men with Saul stood there speechless. They had heard the voice, but they had not seen anyone. Saul got up from the ground, and when he opened his eyes, he could not see a thing. Someone then led him by the hand to Damascus, and for three days he was blind and did not eat or drink.

A follower named Ananias lived in Damascus, and the Lord spoke to him in a vision. Ananias answered, 'Lord, here I am.' The Lord said to him, 'Get up and go to the house of Judas in Straight Street. When you get there, you will find a man named Saul from the city of Tarsus. Saul is praying, and he has seen a vision. He saw a man named Ananias coming to him and putting his hands on him, so that he could see again.'

Ananias replied, 'Lord, a lot of people have told me about the terrible things this man has done to your followers in Jerusalem. Now the chief priests have given him the power to come here and arrest anyone who worships in your name.' The Lord said to Ananias, 'Go! I have chosen him to tell foreigners, kings, and the people of Israel about me. I will show him how much he must suffer for worshipping in my name.'

Ananias left and went into the house where Saul was staying. Ananias placed his hands on him and said, 'Saul, the Lord Jesus has sent me. He is the same one who appeared to you along the road. He wants you to be able to see and to be filled with the Holy Spirit.' Suddenly something like fish scales fell from Saul's eyes, and he could see. He got up and was baptised. Then he ate and felt much better.

For several days Saul stayed with the Lord's followers in Damascus. Soon he went to the Jewish meeting places and started telling people that Jesus is the Son of God. Everyone who heard Saul was amazed and said, 'Isn't this the man who caused so much trouble for those people in Jerusalem who worship in the name of Jesus? Didn't he come here to arrest them and take them to the chief priests?' Saul preached with such power that he completely confused the Jewish people in Damascus, as he tried to show them that Jesus is the Messiah.

ACTS 9:1–22

Bible links

Paul retells the story of his conversion in Acts 22:6–16; 26:12–18.

Key background information for the teacher

Saul was a Pharisee who hated Christians. While travelling to Damascus, he was so transformed by his encounter with Jesus that, even today, people still describe a life-changing event as a 'Damascus road experience'. When Saul became a Christian, he began using the Greek version of his name, Paul. Paul travelled many miles to spread the good news of Jesus and wrote letters to the churches that he established on his travels. A collection of those letters now form a large part of the New Testament.

Suggestions for visual aids and resources

- Some before-and-after pictures, such as extreme makeovers, changed hair styles, angry-to-happy face, and so on
- Light sources
- Photocopies of drama script on pages 31–33

Ideas for exploring the theme

Explore different sources of light with the children. Explain that today's story involves someone who was travelling along a road when he was surrounded by a bright light and heard God speaking to him.

Alternatively, show the before-and-after images. Ask the children if they have seen any TV programmes or adverts that promise to change somebody, such as making them healthier with certain foods, or changing their appearance with hair colouring products or clothing. Point out that some of these things help to change the way we feel about ourselves on the inside.

Say that Christians believe that Jesus can change people's lives for the better on the inside. Christians believe that they can give Jesus the heavy burdens they feel they are carrying and can ask his forgiveness before making a fresh start. Use the angry-to-happy face to reinforce the idea that Christians believe God can change people who trust their lives to him.

The story today is about someone called Saul, whose job it was to arrest people who followed Jesus. Saul was on his way to the town of Damascus when he was suddenly surrounded by a bright light and heard Jesus speaking to him. The experience made a huge difference to his life.

Choose volunteers to enact the story, using the following script. The actors will need to be teachers or competent readers.

— Cast —

Narrator
Saul
Voice of Jesus
Ananias

Narrator: Saul kept on threatening to kill the Lord's followers. He even went to the high priest and asked for letters to the Jewish leaders in Damascus. He did this because he wanted to arrest and take to Jerusalem any man or woman who had accepted the Lord's Way. When Saul had almost reached Damascus, a bright light from heaven suddenly flashed around him. He fell to the ground and heard a voice saying...

Jesus: Saul! Saul! Why are you so cruel to me?

Saul: Who are you?

Jesus: I am Jesus. I am the one you are so cruel to. Now get up and go into the city, where you will be told what to do.

Reproduced with permission from *Assemblies for Spring and Summer Festivals*, BRF 2010 (978 1 84101 701 3)
www.barnabasinschools.org.uk

Narrator: The men with Saul stood there speechless. They had heard the voice, but they had not seen anyone.

Saul: I can't see. Someone help me up.

Narrator: Someone then led Saul by the hand to Damascus. For three days he was blind and did not eat or drink. A man called Ananias lived in Damascus. Jesus spoke to him in a vision.

Ananias: Lord, here I am.

Jesus: Get up and go to the house of Judas in Straight Street. When you get there, you will find a man named Saul from the city of Tarsus. Saul is praying, and he has seen a vision. He saw a man named Ananias coming to him and putting his hands on him, so that he could see again.

Ananias: Lord, a lot of people have told me about the terrible things this man has done to your followers in Jerusalem. Now the chief priests have given him the power to come here and arrest anyone who worships in your name.

Jesus: Go! I have chosen him to tell foreigners, kings and the people of Israel about me. I will show him how much he must suffer for worshipping in my name.

Narrator: Ananias left and went into the house where Saul was staying.

Saul: Who's there? I can't see you. Are you a friend?

Narrator: Ananias placed his hands on him and said...

Ananias: Saul, the Lord Jesus has sent me. He is the same one who appeared to you along the road. He wants you to be able to see and to be filled with the Holy Spirit.

Narrator: Suddenly something like fish scales fell from Saul's eyes, and he could see. He got up and was baptised. Then he ate and felt much better. For several days Saul stayed with Jesus' followers in Damascus.

Saul: I am convinced now that Jesus is the Son of God. He wants me to tell everyone I meet.

Narrator: Soon Saul went to the Jewish meeting places and started telling people about Jesus. Everyone who heard him was amazed and said, 'Isn't this the man who caused so much trouble for those people in Jerusalem who worship in the name of Jesus? Didn't he come here to arrest them and take them to the chief priests?' Saul preached with such power that he completely confused the Jewish people in Damascus, as he tried to show them that Jesus is God's Son.

At the end of the drama, thank the readers and ask them to go back to their seats. Comment that Jesus must have been very upset that his followers were being given such a difficult time, so he met Saul and challenged him. Saul was so amazed by his meeting with Jesus that he was willing to change.

God gave Saul a special job, travelling around the towns and cities of the Mediterranean region to teach people about Jesus. Saul used the Greek version of his name, Paul, as he travelled. Many of the letters he wrote to the churches he established are collected together in the New Testament part of the Bible.

Finish by referring to the before-and-after pictures. Explain that the change in Paul was not on the surface but deep inside, changing the way he thought about God and Jesus. He changed from being the enemy of Jesus' followers to being someone who shared their excitement and spread God's message, whatever the cost.

Reproduced with permission from *Assemblies for Spring and Summer Festivals*, BRF 2010 (978 1 84101 701 3)
www.barnabasinschools.org.uk

Suggestions for songs

All the nations of the earth (CP 14)
Light up the fire (CP 55)

Suggested prayer

Thank you, Jesus, for the difference you made to Saul. Help us to be willing to be changed into better people with your help. Amen

⊕

— Candlemas —

Simeon praises God

Date: 2 February
Theme: The life of Jesus
Curriculum links: Science, RE

Candlemas celebrates the day when the baby Jesus was taken to the temple in Jerusalem to be presented to God. It gives us an opportunity to consider who people thought Jesus was and the work he was born to do.

Because of the connection to temple worship and customs, it is traditional to say a blessing on this day for the use of candles purchased for the coming year. There is a link between this tradition and Jesus' claim to be 'the light for the world' (John 8:12).

Bible story

The time came for Mary and Joseph to do what the Law of Moses says a mother is supposed to do after her baby is born. They took Jesus to the temple in Jerusalem and presented him to the Lord, just as the Law of the Lord says, 'Each firstborn baby boy belongs to the Lord.' The Law of the Lord also says that parents have to offer a sacrifice, giving at least a pair of doves or two young pigeons. So that is what Mary and Joseph did.

At this time a man named Simeon was living in Jerusalem. Simeon was a good man. He loved God and was waiting for God to save the people of Israel. God's Spirit came to him and told him that he would not die until he had seen Christ the Lord. When Mary and Joseph brought Jesus to the temple to do what the Law of Moses says should be done for a new baby, the Spirit told Simeon to go into the temple. Simeon took the baby Jesus in his arms and praised God, 'Lord, I am your servant, and now I can die in peace, because you have kept your promise to me. With my own eyes I have seen what you have done to save your people, and foreign nations will also see this. Your mighty power is a light for all nations, and it will bring honour to your people Israel.'

Jesus' parents were surprised at what Simeon had said. Then he blessed them and told Mary, 'This child of yours will cause many people in Israel to fall and others to stand. The child will be like a warning sign. Many people will reject him, and you, Mary, will suffer as though you had been stabbed by a dagger. But all this will show what people are really thinking.'

The prophet Anna was also there in the temple. She was the daughter of Phanuel from the tribe of Asher, and she was very old. In her youth she had been married for seven years, but her husband died. And now she was eighty-four years old. Night and day she served God in the temple by praying and often going without eating. At that time Anna came in and praised God. She spoke about the child Jesus to everyone who hoped for Jerusalem to be set free.

After Joseph and Mary had done everything that the Law of the Lord commands, they returned home to Nazareth in Galilee. The child Jesus grew. He became strong and wise, and God blessed him.

LUKE 2:22–40

Bible link

'I am the light for the world! Follow me, and you won't be walking in the dark. You will have the light that gives life.'
JOHN 8:12

Key background information for the teacher

2 February is called Candlemas because it was the day on which the supply of candles for the church in the coming year was blessed. It also has a pagan background, as so many Christian festivals do, in that it falls at the midpoint of winter, halfway between the shortest day and the spring equinox. Many people used to believe that the Christmas season lasted for 40 days, until 2 February. Some believed that the weather on this day would be a predictor for the rest of the winter. Conversely, tradition had it that a fine, sunny day meant there was more wintry weather to come, but a cloudy, stormy or wet day meant that the worst weather was over. The belief that the weather could be predicted by what it was like on 2 February was most probably based on close observation of the changing weather patterns by those who worked on the land.

In more recent times, Candlemas has come to celebrate the presentation of the baby Jesus by his parents in the temple in Jerusalem. Jesus would have been named eight days after his birth, although Mary didn't have a problem choosing a name, as the angel had told Mary and Joseph what to call their child. It was the Jewish law that, after having a baby, a woman should attend the synagogue or temple for purification. This rite is still practised in some parts of the world. Purification took place 40 days after a boy was born or 60 days after the birth of a girl.

Suggestions for visual aids and resources

- A candle
- A candle lighter or box of safety matches
- A card showing the words 'Who is Jesus?'

Ideas for exploring the theme

Talk about candles. What are they made of? What do we call the string running down the middle? Light the candle. Explain that, traditionally, Candlemas was the day when candles bought for the church were blessed. Before gas or electric lamps were invented, candles would have been the only source of lighting in churches, schools and homes. Also, for Christians, candles are a reminder that Jesus is the light for the world. Jesus reminds people how much God loves them. He is like a light shining in the darkness.

Show the card with the words 'Who is Jesus?' Candlemas is also the day when Christians remember the baby Jesus being taken to the temple in Jerusalem. In Bible times, it was the tradition that mothers would go to the synagogue or temple after having a baby. In the temple, Mary and Joseph met a man called Simeon and an elderly prophet called Anna. Simeon had been told by God that he would see God's chosen king before he died. When Simeon held the baby Jesus in his arms, he was filled with the power of God. He said, 'Lord, I am your servant, and now I can die in peace, because you have kept your promise to me. With my own eyes I have seen what you have done to save your people, and foreign nations will also see this. Your mighty power is a light for all nations, and it will bring honour to your people Israel.'

Simeon also predicted that people would either love or hate Jesus. They would have to make up their minds about him because he would be such an important person. Anna also felt stirred up by God when she met Mary, Joseph and Jesus. We don't know her exact words but we are told that she praised God for Jesus.

Just like the wise men who visited Jesus, here are some more people who recognised how special he was and realised that the work he would do when he grew up would change the world. He would be like a light in the darkness and everybody would have to make up their minds about who exactly he was. (Hold up the card with the words 'Who is Jesus?')

Suggestions for songs

All the nations of the earth (CP 14)
Light up the fire (CP 55)

Suggested prayer

Dear Jesus, on this day we remember how you were presented at the temple, where some people recognised how special you were. Thank you that, for Christians, you have been a light for the world for hundreds of years. As we look at this candle, we remember how you came to tell people about God's love. Amen

A winning recipe for life

Date: The day before Lent begins
Theme: Special days and celebrations
Curriculum links: PSHE, Literacy, RE

What's the secret to a fulfilled life? For Christians, the answer lies in believing in Jesus as God's Son and in respecting God. Shrove Tuesday is the day before Lent begins and, traditionally, the time when all rich foods and luxuries were used up in order to live a simpler life during Lent. For Christians, a fulfilled life is not based on having lots of possessions or impressing others but on getting our relationship right with God and with our neighbour.

Bible story

After Jesus had made the Sadducees look foolish, the Pharisees heard about it and got together. One of them was an expert in the Jewish Law. So he tried to test Jesus by asking, 'Teacher, what is the most important commandment in the Law?' Jesus answered: Love the Lord your God with all your heart, soul, and mind. This is the first and most important commandment. The second most important commandment is like this one. And it is, 'Love others as much as you love yourself.' All the Law of Moses and the Books of the Prophets are based on these two commandments.

MATTHEW 22:34–40

Bible links

'I came so that everyone would have life, and have it fully.'
JOHN 10:10b

The Lord God has told us what is right and what he demands:
'See that justice is done, let mercy be your first concern, and
humbly obey your God.'
MICAH 6:8

Key background information for the teacher

The name 'Shrove' Tuesday comes from the old word 'shrive',
which means to hear a person's confession. On Shrove Tuesday,
in the Middle Ages, people used to confess their sins so that they
would be forgiven before the season of Lent began. Pancakes are
eaten on this day because they contain fat, butter and eggs, which
were forbidden during Lent. In France, the day is known as Mardi
Gras, which means Fat (or Grease) Tuesday.

Lent is a time of preparation for the festival of Easter. For many
Christians, it is a time when they give up special foods and luxuries
and look for opportunities to do something more positive in God's
service.

In many places, pancake races are held on Shrove Tuesday. The
most famous of these is at Olney in Bedfordshire, and is said to
have originated over 500 years ago, when a woman who was late
for church ran out of the house with a pancake still in her frying
pan. Shrove Tuesday used to be a half-day holiday to allow people
not only to go to church but also to spend time feasting with their
families.

There are several websites giving information about Shrove
Tuesday traditions that have developed in different parts of the UK.

Suggestions for visual aids and resources

- A frying pan
- Flour, eggs and milk (optional)
- A Bible and a cook book

Ideas for exploring the theme

Talk about pancakes. What ingredients are needed to make a pancake? *(Take them out as the children name them.)* How are pancakes made? Why do we eat pancakes on Shrove Tuesday?

Other than food, what might we need a recipe for? Suggest that we could have a recipe for a football match. For example: 'Roll out a pitch of velvet green; add four corner flags to flutter in the breeze and goalposts smothered in netting; pour on two teams of players in different coloured kits, warming up for the match. Spread out the crowds of fans, cheering excitedly for their favourite players; stir in a referee dressed in black with white knobbly knees, a coin in one hand and a whistle in the other. Fold in two linesmen looking strict and impatient to start. Mix well and begin the match!'

Explain that, as Lent is about to start, many Christians will be thinking about how to live a life that will be more pleasing to God. What will need to be given up? Are there bad habits that need to be stopped? Are there activities that need to be taken up instead? It's rather like thinking about the recipe for a better life. Where do people go to find such a recipe? Could they find the answer in a cook book? No! Christians look in the Bible to find the answer. *(Hold up a cook book and a Bible to make the comparison more visual.)*

I wonder what wise advice we can find in the Bible. The Bible tells us that Jesus said, 'I came so that everyone would have life, and have it fully.' During Lent, Christians will often take the opportunity to read the Bible and hear the words of Jesus afresh. Some Christians also spend more time praying and asking God to help them to be more like Jesus.

Christians believe that the Bible contains a kind of recipe for life. Lent is a time to think not just about ourselves but also about how to make the world a fairer place. The prophet Micah reminded us that God wanted his people to obey his laws, to show mercy to people and to act fairly. Wise words!

Suggestions for songs

'Pancakes' in *Songs for Every Season* (Out of the Ark, see page 216 for details)

Suggested prayer

Dear God, thank you for the reminder that you want us to get the best out of our lives. Help us to remember Jesus' words about loving you and our neighbour. Thank you for the Bible with all its stories, events and good advice. Help us to use this time of Lent to pause and think about how we can make life better, not just for ourselves but for others, too. Amen

— Ash Wednesday —

Saying sorry

Date: The first day of Lent
Theme: Special days and celebrations
Curriculum link: PSHE, RE

The period that Christians call Lent lasts in Western churches from Ash Wednesday to the Saturday before Easter Day. (For Roman Catholic Christians, it begins on a Monday but Ash Wednesday is still an important day.) To put the day in its context, see page 51 for an explanation of how the 40 days of Lent are calculated and the various ways Lent is observed by Christians of different traditions.

Bible story

Jonah obeyed the Lord and went to Nineveh. The city was so big that it took three days just to walk through it. After walking for a day, Jonah warned the people, 'Forty days from now, Nineveh will be destroyed!' They believed God's message and set a time when they would go without eating to show their sorrow. Then everyone in the city, no matter who they were, dressed in sackcloth. When the king of Nineveh heard what was happening, he also dressed in sackcloth; he left the royal palace and sat in dust.

JONAH 3:3–6

Bible links

You are kind, God! Please have pity on me. You are always merciful! Please wipe away my sins. Wash me clean from all of my sin and guilt. I know about my sins, and I cannot forget my terrible guilt. You are really the one I have sinned against; I have disobeyed you and have done wrong. So it is right and fair for you to correct and punish me.

I have sinned and done wrong since the day I was born. But you want complete honesty, so teach me true wisdom. Wash me with hyssop until I am clean and whiter than snow. Let me be happy and joyful! You crushed my bones, now let them celebrate. Turn your eyes from my sin and cover my guilt. Create pure thoughts in me and make me faithful again.

PSALM 51:1–10

If we say that we have not sinned, we are fooling ourselves, and the truth isn't in our hearts. But if we confess our sins to God, he can always be trusted to forgive us and take our sins away.

1 JOHN 1:8–9

Key background information for the teacher

Many churches hold special services on Ash Wednesday. The people who attend are often marked with ashes as a sign of sorrow for sin and as a reminder of their mortality. This practice reflects the biblical tradition of covering one's head with ashes and wearing sackcloth as a sign of sorrow.

The priest makes a smudge on the person's forehead or marks the shape of a cross as a reminder of Jesus' death (the same mark is made with water at baptism). Christians believe that Jesus died on a cross to achieve forgiveness for sin and offers his power through the Holy Spirit to help people live according to God's ways. In some churches, the sign is washed off before the people leave as a sign of cleansing, but in other churches believers can leave the sign on their forehead to show that they are taking the love of God and their commitment to him out into the world.

The ashes are usually created by burning palm crosses from the previous year's Palm Sunday service. This reminds believers that the celebration of Jesus' entry into Jerusalem on Palm Sunday led to the pain of the cross before his resurrection. It is a reminder that life is a mixture of celebration and pain. Christians believe that God can guide them through the different stages of life if they walk closely with him. The words typically spoken when the ashes are 'imposed' on people's foreheads are a reminder of the believer's dependence on God.

Suggestions for visual aids and resources

- A palm cross
- Ashes made from burning a palm cross or some newspaper beforehand, or some coal crushed to produce black powder, or black powder paint
- A little cooking oil to help bind the ash together
- A calendar
- Slips of paper showing the following questions:
  - ❖ When is Ash Wednesday?
  - ❖ Why is it called Ash Wednesday?
  - ❖ What are the ashes made from?
  - ❖ What happens on Ash Wednesday?

Ideas for exploring the theme

Show the children some ashes and ask how they have been created. Explain that today is called Ash Wednesday. It is a special day in the Christian calendar but not a day of great celebration.

Take the four slips of paper and ask for a volunteer to read the first question. Ask for a volunteer to read the next question, and so on until all the questions have been read out and answered. Show the palm cross and the ashes at the appropriate moments. Suitable answers to each question are as follows.

1. When is Ash Wednesday?
Ash Wednesday falls six and a half weeks before Easter. It is the first day of Lent—and always on a Wednesday!

2. Why is it called Ash Wednesday?
Ashes have been used for hundreds of years as a symbol of being sorry. In the Bible, it was traditional to rub ashes into your forehead or pour them over your head as a sign that you were sorry and were seeking forgiveness for wrongdoing.

3. What are the ashes made from?
The ashes are made from palm crosses kept from the previous Palm Sunday service. They are burnt and mixed with water or cooking oil to make a paste.

4. What happens on Ash Wednesday?
In church on Ash Wednesday, the priest or minister uses ash to make a smudge or the sign of a cross on people's foreheads as a sign that they are sorry for doing wrong things. People are showing that they want to turn away from doing wrong and live in a way that will please Jesus.

Ask for a volunteer to use the ash on your forehead. Remind the children of what this outward sign means. By letting someone make a cross or smudge of ashes on his or her forehead, the person is showing that he or she wants to live God's way. Conclude by saying that Lent is a time when we can all think about whether there are any habits we want to change, or anything we would like to do to change the world around us for the better.

Suggestions for songs

Give me oil in my lamp (CP 43)
The journey of life (CP 45)
One more step (CP 47, JP 188)
The Lord's Prayer (CP 51, JP 192)
The building song (Ev'rybody's building) (CP 61)

Suggested prayer

Dear God, thank you for the reminder today that you want to give each of us the chance to change and to make the world a better place. Thank you that we can come to you and tell you we are sorry for the things we have done wrong. Thank you that you have promised to travel with us through life. Amen

The Lord's Prayer would also be suitable.

⊹

Forty days and forty nights

Date: Date will vary
Theme: Special days and celebrations
Curriculum links: Maths, RE

This assembly looks at what Lent is, how the period of Lent is calculated and how Christians use the time in various ways to prepare themselves for the celebration of Easter.

Bible story

The Holy Spirit led Jesus into the desert, so that the devil could test him. After Jesus had gone without eating for forty days and nights, he was very hungry. Then the devil came to him and said, 'If you are God's Son, tell these stones to turn into bread.' Jesus answered, 'The Scriptures say: "No one can live only on food. People need every word that God has spoken."'

Next, the devil took Jesus to the holy city and had him stand on the highest part of the temple. The devil said, 'If you are God's Son, jump off. The Scriptures say: "God will give his angels orders about you. They will catch you in their arms, and you won't hurt your feet on the stones." Jesus answered, 'The Scriptures also say, "Don't try to test the Lord your God!"'

Finally, the devil took Jesus up on a very high mountain and showed him all the kingdoms on earth and their power. The devil said to him, 'I will give all this to you, if you will bow down and worship me.' Jesus answered, 'Go away Satan! The

Scriptures say: "Worship the Lord your God and serve only him."' Then the devil left Jesus, and angels came to help him.
MATTHEW 4:1–11

Bible links

'Seven days from now I will send rain that will last for forty days and nights, and I will destroy all other living creatures I have made.'
GENESIS 7:4

The Israelites ate manna for forty years, before they came to the border of Canaan that was a settled land.
EXODUS 16:35–36

Moses... stayed there forty days and nights.
EXODUS 24:17

Straight away God's Spirit made Jesus go into the desert. He stayed there for forty days while Satan tested him. Jesus was with the wild animals, but angels took care of him.
MARK 1:12–13

Key background information for the teacher

The word Lent comes from an old English word meaning 'lengthen'. It is celebrated in spring, when the days begin to get longer. Lent is the period of 40 days in the Christian calendar leading up to Easter, beginning with Ash Wednesday and ending the day before Easter Day.

As well as being a time when people prepare for the celebration of Easter, Lent is used by Christians as a time for reflection when many will examine their own lives and think what changes to their behaviour they could make. As a sign of this intention, many people will fast, going without a meal on a particular day (perhaps giving the money saved to charity) or going without luxuries. This reflects the way Jesus spent time without food in the desert, using his self-discipline and knowledge of scripture to combat the attacks of the devil and reasserting his commitment to follow the path God had set out for him. For other Christians, it is an opportunity to spend more time praying or reading the Bible as a way of getting in closer touch with God's plan for the world and their own lives. For some, it is a time when they consider how to live out their faith more fully, perhaps by getting involved with some voluntary work in their community and so on.

Overall, Lent may be considered as a time of going without certain things in preparation for the festival to come, but also as a time of giving more to others in need. Christians will use Lent in a whole variety of ways, depending on their church tradition.

Western and Eastern churches both observe Lent but count the 40 days differently. In the Western church, Lent begins on Ash Wednesday, the seventh Wednesday before Easter Day, and ends on the day before Easter Day. The Sundays are not counted because they are considered as feast days to remember that Jesus rose from death on a Sunday. In the Eastern church, the Sundays are counted, so Lent (called the Great Lent) begins on the Monday of the seventh week before Easter, ending on the Friday nine days before Easter, and is followed by Holy Week.

Forty has always been a significant number for Jewish people and is used often in the Bible. It can be seen as signifying a prolonged period of time rather than a specific number. Examples include:

- The flood was brought about by 40 days and nights of rain (Genesis 7:4).
- The people of Israel spent 40 years in the wilderness on their journey to find the promised land (Exodus 16:35).
- Moses went without food for 40 days before he received the Ten Commandments on Mount Sinai (Exodus 24:17).

- Jesus spent 40 days in a desert area, preparing to begin his ministry (Mark 1:12–13).

Suggestions for visual aids and resources

- A calendar or a sheet of A1 paper
- A marker pen

Ideas for exploring the theme

Do some sums based on the number 40, such as 8×5, $200 \div 5$, $50 - 10$, $35 + 5$. Ask how many days there are in six weeks, and then in seven weeks. Explain that the period of time that Christians call 'Lent' lasts for 40 days and 40 nights. Counting 40 days for Lent reminds Christians of the length of time that Jesus spent in the desert getting ready to begin his work for God. It was a tough time for him, a time when he was tempted to turn away from the work God wanted him to do and to take an easier path. Perhaps Jesus already knew that this journey would end in his death.

Hold up a calendar or large sheet of paper and show the children how the days are counted back from Easter Day to Ash Wednesday in the Western church. (You will need to point out that other branches of the Church calculate the date differently: see 'Key background information' above.)

Explain that the key to the calculation is to leave out the Sundays, counting six lots of six-day weeks, plus the four days at the very beginning: $(6 \times 6) + 4 = 40$.

Explain that Christians use the 40 days of Lent in many different ways. It used to be a time for teaching new Christians about the faith, before baptising them the day before Easter Day. Those who were already Christians were encouraged to think again about the promises they had made to God and whether they were living in a way that would please God.

For many Christians today, Lent is still a time to have a spiritual 'spring clean' and think about how their journey through life with God is going. Some will try to show the sort of self-discipline that Jesus showed in the desert when he went without food for a long time. They might give up a favourite food, such as chocolate, or go without a meal once a week, perhaps giving the money they would have spent on the food to a charity. Others see it as a time to do something extra—perhaps reading the Bible more, or praying for particular people. They might try to do something useful for others and behave in the loving, caring way that Jesus did. Lent can be an opportunity to take something out of your life, if you're not happy with it, and add something positive instead.

Suggestions for songs

- Forty days and forty nights (HON 145)
- When Jesus walked in Galilee (CP 25)
- Come and praise the Lord our King (CP 21)
- Lord of the dance (CP 22)

Suggested prayer

Dear God, thank you that we can ask you for help with things we would like to change in our lives. During Lent, help us to become better people and to be thankful for all you have given us. Amen

⊕

— Lent (2) —

Water, wine and a wedding

Date: Date will vary
Theme: The life of Jesus
Curriculum link: PSHE

Jesus' first miracle is recorded as having taken place during a wedding. Jesus acted in response to his mother's plea for help. The miracle that followed Mary's request shows the humanity of Jesus as he celebrated a wedding with friends and relations. He responded to the need he saw—something that he often did alongside his teaching.

Bible story

Three days later Mary, the mother of Jesus, was at a **wedding** feast in the village of Cana in Galilee. Jesus and his disciples had also been invited and were there. When the **wine** was all gone, Mary said to Jesus, 'They don't have any more **wine**.' Jesus replied, 'Mother, my time hasn't yet come! You must not tell me what to do.' Mary then said to the servants, 'Do whatever Jesus tells you to do.'

At the feast there were six stone **water** jars that were used by the people for washing themselves in the way that their religion said they must. Each jar held about a hundred litres. Jesus told the servants to fill them to the top with **water**. Then after the jars had been filled, he said, 'Now take some **water** and give it to the man in charge of the feast.' The servants did as Jesus told them, and the man in charge drank some of the **water** that had now turned into **wine**. He did not know where the **wine** had come from, but the servants did. He called the bridegroom over and said, 'The best **wine** is always served first. Then after the guests have had plenty, the other **wine** is served. But you have kept the best until last!'

This was Jesus' first miracle, and he did it in the village of Cana in Galilee. There Jesus showed his glory, and his disciples put their faith in him.

JOHN 2:1–11

Bible link

Jesus worked many other miracles for his disciples, and not all of them are written in this book. But these are written so that you will put your faith in Jesus as the Messiah and the Son of God. If you have faith in him, you will have true life.

JOHN 20:30–31

Key background information for the teacher

The story of the wedding at Cana is recorded only in John's Gospel. In his Gospel, John uses the miracle as a way of pointing to Jesus as the Son of God.

Suggestions for visual aids and resources

• A jug

Ideas for exploring the theme

Explain that you need the children to help with the assembly this morning by joining in with some actions to fit certain words in the story. Practise the following actions to accompany the key words in the Bible story, so that the telling becomes interactive. Practise each action more than once to ensure that the children can respond quickly and their response won't hold up the storytelling.

- **Wedding:** make the sound of a peal of church bells
- **Wine:** drinking action
- **Water:** glugging noise and pouring action

Tell the story using the Bible passage printed above (in which the key words are printed in bold type).

Comment that Jesus knew the wedding would be spoiled if the wine ran out, so he stepped in and helped. What a super way to start his time of teaching, healing and helping! People at the wedding must have really been excited about what he was going to do next.

Suggestions for songs

- Jesus' hands were kind hands (JP 134)
- Come and praise the Lord our king (CP 21)
- Lord of the dance (CP 22)
- When Jesus walked in Galilee (CP 25)
- Praise him (CP 40)

Suggested prayer

Dear God, thank you for Jesus and everything he did to help people. We may not be able to turn water into wine, but help us to do whatever we can when we see someone who needs help. Amen

⊞

— Gladys Aylward —

Don't give up!

Date: 24 February
Theme: Faith in action (later disciples)
Curriculum links: History, Geography

This assembly tells of the life of Gladys Aylward, a missionary to China during the 20th century. She was born on 24 February 1902 and died in 1970.

Bible story

'Go to the people of all nations and make them my disciples. Baptise them in the name of the Father, the Son, and the Holy Spirit, and teach them to do everything I have told you. I will be with you always, even until the end of the world.'

MATTHEW 28:19–20

Bible links

God doesn't take back the gifts he has given or forget about the people he has chosen.

ROMANS 11:29

But he replied, 'My kindness is all you need. My power is strongest when you are weak.' So if Christ keeps giving me his power, I will gladly boast about how weak I am.

2 CORINTHIANS 12:9

We are not preaching about ourselves. Our message is that Jesus Christ is Lord. He also sent us to be your servants. The Scriptures say, 'God commanded light to shine in the dark.' Now God is shining in our hearts to let you know that his glory is seen in Jesus Christ. We are like clay jars in which this treasure is stored. The real power comes from God and not from us.

2 CORINTHIANS 4:5–7

Key background information for the teacher

Gladys Aylward was born at the beginning of the Edwardian period, in 1902. She didn't do very well at school but always enjoyed stories and play-acting or role play. When she was 14, she became a parlourmaid, serving in a wealthy person's house. She became a Christian when she was 18 and, not long afterwards, read a magazine article about how few people in China knew about Jesus. She felt in her heart that she wanted to do something about this. The idea never really went away and years later, when she was 30, she met Mrs Jeannie Lawson, who was looking for an assistant to help her with her Christian work in China. Gladys saved and saved but still didn't have enough money to travel by ship so she decided to set off across land—the hard way! She clearly wasn't going to give up.

When she arrived in the city of Yangchen (south of Beijing) after a long and difficult journey, Gladys planned with Mrs Lawson how they would share the message of Jesus. They had a great idea. Knowing that the city served as an overnight stop for travellers with mules, they decided to restore and repair the building in which they lived, which had once been an inn. It would be a place where they could offer shelter for the mules and a warm bed for the drivers at a fair price. After sharing a meal, they would invite the travellers to listen to stories about Jesus.

To begin with, Mrs Lawson had to do all the storytelling but Gladys realised how important it was to learn the language better.

She worked hard at this so that she could get more involved with the people she met and with the storytelling. In fact, she learned the language well enough to travel round the nearby villages, to help people and to tell them about Jesus. It was here that she discovered many unwanted children, who then came to live with her at her home. The two things Gladys couldn't stop doing were helping people in need and telling them about Jesus.

Suggestions for visual aids and resources

- A map showing the UK and China

Ideas for exploring the theme

Ask the children what is their favourite story about Jesus or that Jesus told. Take some suggestions or offer some possibilities. If some of these stories have been used recently in collective worship or in RE lessons, refer to them. Explain that, today, we will learn about someone who really enjoyed telling and acting out the stories that Jesus told, and even learned Chinese in order to share the love of Jesus with the people she met.

Use the biography in the 'Key background information' above, then say that Gladys Aylward is a great example of someone who served other people, helping wherever she could. She isn't famous for being clever or strong but for being determined and for letting God use her. She didn't see herself as very special but she believed that, with God's help, all sorts of things became possible.

Suggestions for songs

- Spirit of God (CP 63)
- I, the Lord of sea and sky (HON 235)
- Tell out, my soul (HON 467)
- Give me oil in my lamp (CP 43)

- When I needed a neighbour (CP 65, JP 275)
- The journey of life (CP 45)
- One more step (CP 47, JP 188)
- The building song (Ev'rybody's building) (CP 61)
- Cross over the road (CP 70)
- Make me a channel (OSS 81, JP 161)
- Be bold, be strong (TS 38, KS 17)

Suggested prayer

Thank you for what we can learn from the life of Gladys Aylward, who relied on you for help. Thank you for the stories of Jesus that she told and that we still enjoy hearing today. Thank you that they remind us of your great love for us and what a mighty God you are.

Dearest Lord, teach me to be generous; teach me to serve you as you deserve; to give and not to count the cost; to fight and not to heed the wounds; to labour and not to seek to rest; to give of myself and not to ask for reward, except the reward of knowing that I am doing your will. Amen

PRAYER OF SAINT IGNATIUS LOYOLA

⊕

— David —

Get into training for God

Date: 1 March
Theme: Saints of Britain
Curriculum links: Science, PSHE

This assembly explores the idea that Christians should be in training to serve God and the people around them. In order to do this, they need to look after their bodies and minds, develop their faith and practise using the gifts God has given them, within the church community and also in sharing the good news with people around them.

Bible story

You know that many runners enter a race, and only one of them wins the prize. So run to win! Athletes work hard to win a crown that cannot last, but we do it for a crown that will last for ever. I don't run without a goal. And I don't box by beating my fists in the air. I keep my body under control and make it my slave, so I won't lose out after telling the good news to others.

1 CORINTHIANS 9:24–27

Bible links

You know that your body is a temple where the Holy Spirit lives. The Spirit is in you and is a gift from God. You are no longer your own. God paid a great price for you. So use your body to honour God.

1 CORINTHIANS 6:19–20

I have not yet reached my goal, and I am not perfect. But Christ has taken hold of me. So I keep on running and struggling to take hold of the prize. My friends, I don't feel that I have already arrived. But I forget what is behind, and I struggle for what is ahead. I run towards the goal, so that I can win the prize of being called to heaven. This is the prize that God offers because of what Christ Jesus has done.

PHILIPPIANS 3:12–14

Key background information for the teacher

David is the patron saint of Wales, the country in which he grew up and established monasteries after a ten-year period of study. He is well known for his rule of life, which included abstinence from meat and alcohol. He was a powerful speaker, arguing against false teaching, and was eventually made head of the church in Wales.

Naturally, with someone who lived many centuries ago, it is hard to separate fact from legend. However, it is undisputed that he lived in Wales in the sixth century and was the son of an aristocratic family. He was taught by a monk called Paulinus and was one of the early saints who helped to spread Christianity among the pagan Celtic tribes of Western Britain.

David was based at Menevia, which became the large village now called St David's in Pembrokeshire (granted city status by our present Queen because of its cathedral and its significance to Welsh people and indeed Christians throughout the UK). For many years, St David's has been an important place of pilgrimage. Four visits to David's burial place were considered worth the same as two to Rome or one to Jerusalem.

Suggestions for visual aids and resources

Either:
• Cards showing the words 'carnivore', 'herbivore' and 'omnivore'.

- A daffodil, a leek or pictures of Saint David (Google images for St David's Day))

Or:
- Pictures of famous sports people
- Different footwear, including trainers

Ideas for exploring the theme

There are two ways you could begin this assembly. Choose whichever you think will be received better by your children, or use both if the assembly is to be presented to the whole school by a class of children. The assembly could start and finish with Welsh music, such as harp music or a folksong such as 'David of the White Rock' or 'Men of Harlech'.

For older children, show the cards with the words 'herbivore', 'carnivore' and 'omnivore', terms that should be known by children at the top end of Key Stage Two. Discuss their meanings and ask for examples of animals that fit into each category. Explain that although most humans are omnivores, many adults choose not to eat certain types of food for a variety of reasons—perhaps to improve their health, to lose weight, or because of concerns about the care of animals or the pesticides used on crops. Explain that we are going to look at a famous Christian who chose to give up eating meat and drinking alcohol in order to live a healthy life, so that he would be fit and ready to work for God. His name was David and he is the special (patron) saint for Wales.

Some people have suggested that the leek was associated with Wales because David was a vegetarian. Later on, the daffodil became more popular as an emblem, probably because it was easier to wear and less smelly than a leek. The red dragon has also become a symbol of Wales. It is pictured on the flag that is flown all over Wales on St David's Day. (Show visuals to the children.)

For younger children, show pictures of famous sports people and ask them to identify the sport, the person or the team. Alternatively, you could look at a variety of different footwear and ask what it is used for. Make sure you include a pair of trainers. Discuss how sports people train to be fit.

Introduce the story of David, a Welsh monk who studied hard to learn all he could about God and then wanted to share his knowledge with others. David gathered groups of monks around him and set up ten or more monasteries in order to organise and train them. In each monastery, the rule was that the monks could drink only water and eat vegetables and bread as they studied and worked. (Some histories of David suggest that although he drank only water, he did allow the other monks to drink milk.)

David was put in charge of the church in Wales because he knew the Bible well, spoke plainly and could explain the message of God's love clearly, putting people right if they had got it in a muddle. David is reported as saying that we don't have to go searching for great things to do but can 'do little things' for God instead.

In the Bible, Paul teaches that all Christians should live as if they are in a great race, trying to serve God and the people around them as well as they possibly can. You could read 1 Corinthians 9:24–27 to reinforce the point.

Suggestions for songs

• Spirit of God (CP 63)

Suggested prayer

Dear God, thank you for the example of David. Help us to look after our bodies and keep fit and healthy. Help all your followers today to learn how to serve you better. Help them to explain clearly to others how much you love everyone and want to help them live better lives, so that they will be really happy. Amen

— George Müller —

Reliable God

Date: 10 March
Theme: Faith in action (later disciples)
Curriculum links: History, PSHE

George Müller is a prime example of someone who relied on God and expected God to meet the needs of others he prayed for.

Bible story

When you pray, don't be like those show-offs who love to stand up and pray in the meeting places and on the street corners. They do this just to look good. I can assure you that they already have their reward. When you pray, go into a room alone and close the door. Pray to your Father in private. He knows what is done in private, and he will reward you. When you pray, don't talk on and on as people do who don't know God. They think God likes to hear long prayers. Don't be like them. Your Father knows what you need before you ask.

MATTHEW 6:5–8

Bible links

Give us our food for today.

MATTHEW 6:11

The man replied, 'The Scriptures say, "Love the Lord your God with all your heart, soul, strength, and mind." They also say, "Love your neighbours as much as you love yourself."'

LUKE 10:27

But Jesus said, 'Let the children come to me, and don't try to stop them! People who are like these children belong to God's kingdom.'

MATTHEW 19:14

'Whenever you did it for any of my people, no matter how unimportant they seemed, you did it for me.'

MATTHEW 25:40

Key background information for the teacher

George Müller was a Christian worker who felt called to respond to the needs he saw in society around him. His faith resulted in action to help others. He was also a man who kept in close touch with God by praying, and he had high expectations that if he was about God's business, God would help him to get it done.

George was born on 27 September 1805 and died on 10 March 1898, so he lived right across the later Georgian and Victorian periods—a time when social care and provisions for the health and welfare for children were at an embryonic stage. With many adults dying in poverty or from disease, it was not surprising to find so many children orphaned, especially in the cities. Workhouses were set up to help, but they offered a grim, harsh existence.

Prayer was a backbone of George Müller's life. The regular time he spent talking to God not only changed him but also enabled him to sense how, in particular, he should serve God. He believed that, through prayer, God could change situations.

Suggestions for visual aids and resources

- Some bread and milk
- A table and chairs (optional)
- Some empty plates (optional)

Ideas for exploring the theme

People once asked Jesus how they should pray, and his answer was to say the words that have become known as the Lord's Prayer. If the children are familiar with this prayer, ask them to say it now. Explain that it includes lots of ideas, such as telling God that we want his wishes to be fulfilled, asking his help for the difficulties we face and so on. Today, though, we are going to focus on one line in it: 'Give us today our daily bread.'

Bread is a basic food and most of us are lucky enough to be able to eat much more than just basic food. In some countries, water and simple food, like bread or rice, are all that children have, day after day. In some parts of the world, even these are luxuries, and aid workers have to bring in basic foods to help people survive.

Explain that Jesus was saying that we all have basic needs for food, water, clothes, shelter and medicine. Christians believe that Jesus wants us to pray to God for his help if we or other people are not having these needs met.

Show the bread and milk at this point and explain that today we are going to hear about someone who lived at the time of Queen Victoria. He saw children in great need and felt that it was his duty to do something to help. The problem was, he didn't have a lot of his own money to give them, but that didn't stop him! He knew from his own experience that God could supply his own basic needs. The man's name was George Müller and he lived in Bristol. It was a busy city and there were many orphans on the streets (orphans are children without any parents). Some got taken to workhouses but often didn't survive the harsh conditions there.

George had an idea. He would rent a house and equip it so that he could take some of these children off the streets and look after them. Not only would he feed and clothe them but he would also teach them how to earn a living with simple trades. After a while, he set up more houses, but there always seemed to be children waiting for a place to live. We might have expected him to ask lots of people for money, rather like organised charities do today, but George decided that if God wanted him to do this work, he could ask God to provide what was needed.

Money and gifts arrived as he needed them, and stories are recorded of some unusual occurrences. For example, one morning the children arrived for breakfast to find empty plates. The children were relying on George, but George was relying on God. He prayed, thanking God that he would provide what they all needed to eat.

(Ask for two volunteers to act out the roles of the baker and milkman while you tell the story. If you wish, extend the role play by having a table set up, with children waiting to eat in front of empty plates.)

There was a knock at the door. There stood the baker, who explained that he had woken up in the middle of the night and thought of the children being cared for by George. He sensed that God was telling him to bake extra bread and deliver it to them in time for breakfast. The children had just started to enjoy the bread when there was another knock at the door. This time it was a milkman, who said, 'My milk cart has broken down outside and I need to empty the wagon to repair it. Could you use the milk for the children?'

Of course, George thanked the milkman and then said a 'thank you' prayer to God for yet another example of his provision for the children.

Some people might see these occurrences as luck or coincidence, but people who believe in God see them as examples of how God answered George Müller's prayers and made unusual things happen.

Comment that, for George, prayer was a very important part of life. He believed that as we pray, God can guide us on our journey through life. He believed that God will sometimes give us special jobs but that we should do everything as if we were doing it to serve God. He believed that prayer can change things around us, as well as changing ourselves as we spend more time with God.

Suggestions for songs

- Our Father, who art in heaven (CP 51)
- The journey of life (CP 45)
- One more step (CP 47, JP 188)
- The building song (Ev'rybody's building) (CP 61)
- When I needed a neighbour (CP 65, JP 275)
- Cross over the road (CP 70)

Suggested prayer

Dear God, thank you for the example of George Müller, who saw a job to be done and got on with it. Thank you that he also showed how important it is to pray and to let you guide our lives. Help us to be the sort of people who really enjoy changing the world around us for the better. Amen

The Lord's Prayer would also be suitable.

— Patrick —

Slave, shepherd, saint

Date: 17 March
Theme: Saints of Britain
Curriculum link: History

God didn't waste any of Patrick's experience. Once he committed his life to God, God used the things that had happened to him and the people he had met to a greater purpose, although life for Patrick certainly continued to bring both excitement and challenge.

Patrick's writings include the following confession:

I came to the Irish people to preach the Gospel and endure the taunts of unbelievers, putting up with reproaches about my earthly pilgrimage, suffering many persecutions, even bondage, and losing my birthright of freedom for the benefit of others.

If I am worthy, I am ready also to give up my life, without hesitation and most willingly, for Christ's name. I want to spend myself for that country, even in death, if the Lord should grant me this favour.

It is among that people that I want to wait for the promise made by him, who assuredly never tells a lie. He makes this promise in the Gospel: 'They shall come from the east and west and sit down with Abraham, Isaac and Jacob.' This is our faith: believers are to come from the whole world.

Bible story

Jesus came to them and said: I have been given all authority in heaven and on earth! Go to the people of all nations and make them my disciples. Baptise them in the name of the Father, the Son, and the Holy Spirit, and teach them to do everything I have told you. I will be with you always, even until the end of the world.

MATTHEW 28:18–20

Bible link

Come to Jesus Christ. He is the living stone that people have rejected, but which God has chosen and highly honoured. And now you are living stones that are being used to build a spiritual house. You are also a group of holy priests, and with the help of Jesus Christ you will offer sacrifices that please God.

1 PETER 2:4–5

Key background information for the teacher

Patrick was born around AD387–390 in either northern England or southern Scotland. His name at the time was Maewyn, Patrick being the name that was given him by the Church later on. He was kidnapped as a teenager, shipped to Ireland and given work as a shepherd in the mountains. It is said that he spent a great deal of time in prayer and sometimes heard God's voice. He was told when to escape and to return to Britain.

Patrick studied in continental Europe, becoming a priest and later a bishop. He was sent by the Pope to evangelise England, then Ireland. Most of his later life was spent in Ireland and, after 33 years, it was noted that the majority of the people there believed in Jesus. Not surprisingly, he is regarded as the patron saint of Ireland. The shamrock is often pictured as an emblem of Ireland because it is said that Patrick used it to explain the Trinity. He is sometimes credited with ridding Ireland of snakes, but no one is sure that there were any poisonous ones in the country anyway. It could be that the snake is a symbol of Ireland's pagan past being driven out as Christianity became the dominant faith, as it has been ever since.

Some of Patrick's writings have survived and some of his prayers are still used today. St Patrick's Day is celebrated on 17 March throughout Ireland and many interesting traditions have developed over the centuries. Some of the country's pagan past seems to have resurfaced, with mischievous leprechauns often pictured as part of Irish folklore and celebrations on St Patrick's Day. If you would like to extend the assembly theme into class work and research, you will find several websites dedicated to St Patrick's Day celebrations, including some with fun games and puzzles.

Suggestions for visual aids and resources

- An outline drawing of a shamrock
- A picture of St Patrick

Ideas for exploring the theme

Encourage children to respond to the following key words as you tell the story of Patrick's life. Apart from 'king', all the key words begin with the letter 's', but not all the words beginning with 's' in the text have an action, so the children will need to stay alert. Key words are shown in bold in the story below.

- **King**: bow or put crown on head
- **Slave**: lock wrists together
- **Shepherd** or **sheep**: baa
- **Study** or **student**: open hands like a book
- **Sailors**, **sail** or **ship**: ripple hand across in front of you
- **Spread**: place hands together flat in a book shape, and then separate widely
- **Saint**: place hands together as in prayer

Nobody knows exactly where Patrick was born but it is likely to have been in either northern England or southern Scotland. As a teenager he was kidnapped and taken to Ireland as a **slave**, where he was put to work as a **shepherd** by a landowner called Meluic. He found comfort from the Christian faith during these bleak years looking after **sheep**. After six years he heard a voice telling him that the time had come to escape and that a **ship** was waiting to take him home. Sure enough, after a journey of 200 miles to Wexford he found a **ship** waiting, although at first he was turned away by the captain. He prayed for God's help and guidance and heard the **sailors** calling him back. He travelled home, but not before being captured again, this time for only two months. He decided to **study** and **sailed** to France to do this, returning to Britain as a priest. Then one day he heard a voice while praying, which begged him to come back. 'Come and walk once more amongst us,' the voice said.

Patrick understood this as an instruction to **sail** to Ireland. He knew that if he could get the go-ahead from the High **King** of Tara, the most powerful man in Ireland, he would be free to travel about and **spread** the message about Jesus. He decided to attract attention by lighting a massive fire at the start of spring. This broke the rules because the **king**'s fire was always the first to be lit. The **king** raced to the scene and was met by Patrick and his friends, all dressed simply, ready not to fight but to talk. Patrick had got the **king**'s attention and the meeting he wanted. He stressed that he was there not to take power from the **king** but to spread the good news about Jesus. The **king** turned out to be Laoghaire, the son of the man who had taken Patrick captive as a **slave** many before.

The **king** greeted Patrick warmly at his court the next day and asked him to explain about the God he served. Patrick explained that he believed and trusted in one God, but that

God could be worshipped as Father, Son and Holy Spirit. The time he'd spent as a **student** helped Patrick to think quickly. He had noticed a three-leaved plant, a type of clover that the Irish called shamrock, and used it to explain that just as there are three leaves on one stem, so it is perfectly possible to believe in one God in three ways. The **king** was impressed enough by Patrick to allow him to travel through the land, spreading the Christian message, although the **king** did not change his own beliefs.

Many people gathered to listen to Patrick and believed his message, becoming Christians, so much so that the Christians in Ireland outnumbered the believers in any other faith. It is said that the Pope in Rome was very pleased with Patrick for his hard work. After his death on 17 March 461, at the great age of 76, Patrick was named a **saint** by the Church.

Explain that Patrick is a very good example of someone who studied hard to learn as much as he could. He used all the experiences he had in life to learn more about people and himself. He also had great ideas to explain Christian beliefs to other people. Just like Jesus, he used very ordinary examples from the world around him in his teaching, the most famous being the three leaves of the shamrock, which reminded him of God as Father, Son and Spirit.

Patrick wanted God to be involved in every part of his life, which must have been quite hard to do, but he felt that God deserved this involvement because he had shown such great love to us through the life and death of Jesus. This idea comes through very strongly in a famous prayer that Patrick wrote, which we can listen to today (see below).

Suggestions for songs

- Spirit of God (CP 63)
- Light up the fire (CP 55)
- For all the saints (HON 134)

Suggested prayer

Christ shield me this day:
Christ with me,
Christ before me,
Christ behind me,
Christ in me,
Christ beneath me,
Christ above me,
Christ on my right,
Christ on my left,
Christ when I lie down,
Christ when I arise,
Christ in the heart of every person who thinks of me,
Christ in every eye that sees me,
Christ in the ear that hears me.
Amen

As this prayer is being read out, children could mime the different actions with their hands. There is a slightly different version in *Multi-Sensory Prayer* by Sue Wallace (SU, 2004, pp. 25–26), with actions illustrated by photos.

— Mothering Sunday —

Mothers' Day

Date: Usually the second or third Sunday in March
Theme: Special days and celebrations
Curriculum link: PSHE

Christians believe that God planned for people to live in families and that he has a particular place in his heart for those whose family life has gone wrong. There are many examples of people crying out to God and his people for help with their family situations. Today's Bible story features a widow and her sons who come to Elisha for help, and shows God intervening on behalf of the family. For Christians, God is not so worried about the shape that a family might take as about the care that is shown by adults for children, and by children for adults, based on love and respect.

Remember to be sensitive to the various family patterns of the children, especially for anyone who has suffered a recent bereavement or break-up. Although it was originally a church festival, celebrating the family of the church and of the churches linked within a local area, Mothering Sunday is an ideal opportunity to celebrate the role that mothers play in our families.

Bible story

One day the widow of one of the Lord's prophets said to Elisha, 'You know that before my husband died, he was a follower of yours and a worshipper of the Lord. But he owed a man some money, and now that man is on his way to take my two sons as his slaves.' 'Perhaps there's something I can do to help,' Elisha said. 'What do you have in your house?' 'Sir, I have nothing but a small bottle of olive oil.' Elisha told her, 'Ask your neighbours for their empty jars. And after you've borrowed as many as you can, go home and shut the door behind you and your sons. Then begin filling the jars with oil and set each one aside as you fill it.' The woman left.

Later, when she and her sons were back inside their house, the two sons brought her the jars, and she began filling them. At last, she said to one of her sons, 'Bring me another jar.' 'We don't have any more,' he answered, and the oil stopped flowing from the small bottle.

After she told Elisha what had happened, he said, 'Sell the oil and use part of the money to pay what you owe the man. You and your sons can live on what is left.'

2 KINGS 4:1–7

Bible link

Invest in truth and wisdom, discipline and good sense, and don't part with them. Make your father truly happy by living right and showing sound judgment. Make your parents proud, especially your mother.

PROVERBS 23:23–25

Key background information for the teacher

Elisha was trained by the great prophet Elijah. He took over the leadership of a group of prophets whose job it was to keep reminding God's people what God expected of them. Elisha felt that it was his duty to care for those who became his followers and, by extension, for their families.

The life of a prophet was simple, without luxuries and somewhat sacrificial, so it is not surprising that the dead man's widow had no savings and faced seeing her sons taken away as slaves to pay her family's debts. Elisha knew from his own understanding of God and God's laws that orphans and widows should be looked after. He trusted that God would answer his prayers and so he gave the widow instructions to follow.

It is typical of a prophet that he might give some rather odd instructions, but the other person is called to trust that the prophet knows what he is doing and that the results will be worth the effort involved. The story of Elisha and Naaman, in 2 Kings 5:1–19, is another example. Perhaps Elisha also remembered hearing how his teacher, Elijah, had helped a widow and her son at Zarephath (1 Kings 17:8–16).

Other biblical mothers include Hagar, the slave of Abraham who bore him a child (Genesis 16:1–16); Jochebed, the mother of Moses (Exodus 2:1–3); Hannah, the mother of Samuel, who gave her promised child as a thank-offering to work at the temple (1 Samuel 1:20–28); the Canaanite woman who, despite being outside the Jewish community, begged Jesus to help her daughter, believing that he had the power to do so (Matthew 15:21–28); and, of course, Jesus' own mother, Mary, who sang a song of praise to God for allowing her to become the mother of his promised Saviour (Luke 1:46–55). Her cousin Elizabeth, on meeting the newly pregnant Mary, cried out, 'God has blessed you more than any other woman! He has also blessed the child you will have. Why should the mother of my Lord come to me?' (Luke 1:42-43). These famous Bible mothers could be studied for a class presentation, if appropriate.

Suggestions for visual aids and resources

- A bottle of cooking oil
- Some small jars, mostly full of oil
- A box in which to hide the jars

Ideas for exploring the theme

Ask the children to hold up the right number of fingers for the people in their families. Comment that there are clearly lots of different family sizes and each family is different. Explain that Mothers' Day is the day when we show special appreciation for our mothers but, for Christians, this day is also a time to celebrate families in all sorts of shapes and sizes. Christians believe that God wants everyone to be part of his family.

Today we are going to hear about a family who were going through a very tough patch. The father had died and left a wife and two sons. In those days, if someone owed lots of money, the children could be taken away to work in order to settle the debt. They would have to serve as slaves.

This particular father had worked with Elisha, a special leader of God's people, so when he died the children's mother went to Elisha and begged him for help.

Elisha knew that God always wanted widows and children to be looked after, and God gave him a plan to help. He asked the woman if she had anything to sell in order to raise the money needed. All she had was a small bottle of oil. *(Show the bottle of oil.)* She kept pouring oil from the bottle into a series of jars as her sons brought them to her, until she ran out of jars. Then the bottle ran out of oil. *(Bring out the jars of oil one at a time.)*

The widow and her sons were amazed at where all the oil had come from, but she praised God that she now had something to sell to pay off her debts. In fact, she found that once she had paid the money she owed, she still had money left over to buy what she needed for her family to live on.

Explain that God gave the widow a miraculous way out of her problem. God loves families and appreciated how much this mother cared for her children. Christians believe that God cares for everyone, rich or poor, whether they live with their mum and dad or just one parent, whether life is easy or difficult. The Bible tells us that Jesus grew up in a family home with his mother Mary, her husband Joseph and their other children. Christians believe that Jesus will always listen to our prayers for families who need help. For Christians, God has also given the church family, who are ready to support and help anyone who is having problems.

Suggestions for songs

- I'm special (JP 106, KS 162, TS 222)
- Now thank we all our God (HON 354)
- For the beauty of the earth (CP 11)
- Father God, I wonder (HON 119)
- Bind us together (HON 60)
- Let there be love (HON 298)
- Don't forget (Mothers' Day song) (*Songs for Every Easter* CD pack, Out of the Ark)

Suggested prayer

Thank you for all those who care for us, especially our mums and grandmas. Thank you, Jesus, that you grew up in a family and know what it is like—that it is sometimes tough but never dull. Thank you for Mary, who cared for you as you grew up. Please be with our families, whatever they are like, and especially be with anyone finding life at home difficult at the moment. Amen

— The annunciation —

An unexpected visitor

Date: 25 March
Theme: The life of Jesus
Curriculum links: Drama, RE

For Christians, the annunciation is one of the most important moments in human history, alongside the resurrection of Jesus. What an amazing moment for Mary, when she was invited to accept the indwelling of God within her, to become the human mother of the promised Messiah! Her personality, her betrothal to someone in the lineage of King David (some traditions suggest that Mary was of the same ancestry) and the fact that she was related to the mother of John the Baptist were all important features of God's choice.

Bible story

God sent the angel Gabriel to the town of Nazareth in Galilee with a message for a virgin named Mary. She was engaged to Joseph from the family of King David. The angel greeted Mary and said, 'You are truly blessed! The Lord is with you.' Mary was confused by the angel's words and wondered what they meant. Then the angel told Mary, 'Don't be afraid! God is pleased with you, and you will have a son. His name will be Jesus. He will be great and will be called the Son of God Most High. The Lord God will make him king, as his ancestor David was. He will rule the people of Israel for ever, and his kingdom will never end.'

Mary asked the angel, 'How can this happen? I am not married!' The angel answered, 'The Holy Spirit will come down

to you, and God's power will come over you. So your child will
be called the holy Son of God. Your relative Elizabeth is also
going to have a son, even though she is old. No one thought she
could ever have a baby, but in three months she will have a son.
Nothing is impossible for God!'

Mary said, 'I am the Lord's servant! Let it happen as you have
said.' And the angel left her.

LUKE 1:26–38

Bible link

The Word became a human being and lived here with us. We
saw his true glory, the glory of the only Son of the Father. From
him all the kindness and all the truth of God have come down
to us.

JOHN 1:14

Key background information for the teacher

The feast of the annunciation, celebrated on 25 March, is one of the
most important in the Christian calendar. It celebrates the moment
when Jesus was conceived in the womb of his mother, Mary. The
biblical account in Luke 1:26–38 describes the news given by the
angel Gabriel to Mary that she was to become the mother of God's
Son. For many Catholic Christians, it is also a feast day on which
they remember that God holds human life sacred, having made it
holy by choosing to be born as Jesus through a human woman.

Some other lessons that can be drawn from this important event
are the Christian understanding of the Trinity—Father, Son and
Holy Spirit—and the important role played by angels as God's
messengers.

The words with which Gabriel greeted Mary have become a
Roman Catholic prayer called the Hail Mary, which reflects the
angel's greeting: 'You are truly blessed! The Lord is with you.'

Mary's humility and trust in God's plan for her life are enshrined in her reply, 'I am the Lord's servant! Let it happen as you have said.'

Suggestions for visual aids and resources

- A picture or computer image of the annunciation
- Photocopies of the script on pages 84–85

Ideas for exploring the theme

Tell some knock-knock jokes, such as:

Knock, knock!
Who's there?
Stopwatch.
Stopwatch who?
Stopwatch you're doing right now!

Knock, knock!
Who's there?
Cash.
Cash who?
No, thank you, I prefer peanuts!

Knock, knock!
Who's there?
Zippy.
Zippy who?
Zippy dee-doo-dah! Zippy dee-ay!

Knock, knock!
Who's there?
Ken.
Ken who?
Ken I come in? It's freezing out here!

Knock, knock!
Who's there?
Barry.
Barry who?
Barry the treasure where no one will find it!

Today's assembly is about someone who didn't knock but came in anyway—an angel! It's a long time until Christmas, but today we remember an event that is, in fact, part of the Christmas story. It takes approximately 40 weeks for a baby to grow inside his or her mother until the time comes to be born. Forty weeks is about nine months, and in nine months' time it will be 25 December—Christmas Day, the day when we celebrate the birth of Jesus. We can't be sure of the exact date of the very first Christmas or the date when the angel visited Mary, but Christians have chosen these two dates as a reminder of these important events.

Imagine how shocked Mary must have felt when an angel appeared—and her surprise would become greater when she heard his message.

Choose volunteers to enact the story, using the following script.

— Cast —

Narrator
Gabriel
Mary

Narrator: God sent the angel Gabriel to the town of Nazareth in Galilee with a message for a virgin named Mary. She was engaged to Joseph from the family of King David. The angel greeted Mary and said…

Gabriel: You are truly blessed! The Lord is with you.

Narrator: Mary was confused by Gabriel's words and wondered what they meant. Then the angel told her…

Gabriel: Don't be afraid! God is pleased with you, and you will have a son. His name will be Jesus. He will be great and will be called the Son of God Most High. The Lord God will make him king, as his ancestor David was. He will rule the people of Israel for ever, and his kingdom will never end.

Narrator: Mary asked the angel...

Mary: How can this happen? I am not married!

Gabriel: The Holy Spirit will come down to you, and God's power will come over you. So your child will be called the holy Son of God. Your relative Elizabeth is also going to have a son, even though she is old. No one thought she could ever have a baby, but in three months she will have a son. Nothing is impossible for God!

Mary: I am the Lord's servant! Let it happen as you have said.

Narrator: Then the angel left her.

Thank the actors and ask them to return to their seats.

Explain that Christians believe that God likes people to say 'yes' to him and to be willing to obey him. Mary was just an ordinary person but she was willing to do as he asked. Mary is a great example of a humble person who trusted her future into God's hands. For Christians, nothing is impossible for God: he is a God of surprises!

Suggestions for songs

• The angel Gabriel from heaven came (HON 471)
• Gabriel's song (Mary, Mary, you are the one) (see page 212)

Suggested prayer

Dear God, thank you for Mary, who accepted your invitation to be Jesus' mother. Thank you for her example of humility and obedience as she gave her future to you and trusted you for what was to happen. Help us to learn from her about how trustworthy you are and to remember the words of the angel, that with you 'nothing is impossible'. Amen

— Palm Sunday —

Hosanna to the Son of David

Date: The Sunday before Easter Day
Theme: The life of Jesus
Curriculum links: History, RE

This assembly is based on the idea of welcoming and greeting someone special. This theme links to the arrival of Jesus in Jerusalem and the way people used palm branches and cloaks for an impromptu celebration, greeting Jesus as the expected Messiah.

Bible story

When Jesus and his disciples came near Jerusalem, he went to Bethphage on the Mount of Olives and sent two of them on ahead. He told them, 'Go into the next village, where you will at once find a donkey and her colt. Untie the two donkeys and bring them to me. If anyone asks why you are doing that, just say, "The Lord needs them." Straight away he will let you have the donkeys.'

So God's promise came true, just as the prophet had said, 'Announce to the people of Jerusalem: "Your king is coming to you! He is humble and rides on a donkey. He comes on the colt of a donkey."' The disciples left and did what Jesus had told them to do. They brought the donkey and its colt and laid some clothes on their backs. Then Jesus got on.

Many people spread clothes in the road, while others put down branches which they had cut from trees. Some people walked ahead of Jesus and others followed behind. They were all shouting, 'Hooray for the Son of David! God bless the one who comes in the name of the Lord. Hooray for God in heaven above!'

When Jesus came to Jerusalem, everyone in the city was excited and asked, 'Who can this be?' The crowd answered, 'This is Jesus, the prophet from Nazareth in Galilee.'

MATTHEW 21:1–11

Bible links

God bless the one who comes in the name of the Lord! We praise you from here in the house of the Lord. The Lord is our God, and he has given us light! Start the celebration! March with palm branches all the way to the altar.

PSALM 118:26–27

Everyone in Jerusalem, celebrate and shout! Your king has won a victory, and he is coming to you. He is humble and rides on a donkey; he comes on the colt of a donkey.

ZECHARIAH 9:9

Key background information for the teacher

Hosanna is a Hebrew word meaning 'save', which became an exclamation of praise. By calling Jesus 'the Son of David', the crowds were acknowledging that he was the promised Messiah, who was prophesied to be from David's family line.

'Blessed is he who comes in the name of the Lord' is now a sung response in the liturgy for Holy Communion and comes from Psalm 118:26. Verse 27 of the same psalm mentions palm branches, giving a clear prophetic link to the way people celebrated Jesus' entry into Jerusalem. Psalm 118:22, 'The stone that the builders tossed aside has now become the most important stone', is also quoted elsewhere in the Bible as a reminder that Jesus was the expected Christ and, despite being rejected by many people, became the cornerstone of a new building, a new way for God to build his kingdom on earth (for example, Mark 12:10; 1 Peter 2:7). Jesus' choice of a donkey for transport is an echo of the prophecy in the book of Zechariah, a statement of his desire to come as a peaceful leader. Jesus deliberately chose to ride on a donkey to let people know who he believed himself to be, but the use of palms can be regarded as a spontaneous action on the part of the crowds.

In the way that he records the events of the entry into Jerusalem, Matthew is clearly showing that Jesus was the fulfilment of people's expectations—the awaited Messiah, the Saviour of God's people.

Suggestions for visual aids and resources

- A picture of a palm tree, a donkey and a palm cross
- A picture of a king or queen, or similar well-known people
- A card showing the words, 'Who can this be?'

Ideas for exploring the theme

Ask the children to tell you the names of famous people who are alive today. You might want to help them by showing a celebrity magazine or pictures. Ask them to imagine that one of these famous people, a 'Very Important Person', might find the time to visit your school. How would you get ready? For example, you might put out a red carpet, contact the local newspaper or TV station, clean the windows, get dressed up, brush your hair, make a banner, practise bowing or write a speech. But what if you weren't expecting the visit or only had a few minutes to prepare? (Give the children one minute to talk to a neighbour before sharing their answers with the whole group.)

Introduce the events of Palm Sunday, telling the story in your own words or reading the biblical account (see above). Point out how Jesus surprised the people of Jerusalem by choosing to ride on a donkey. This would have reminded the people that God's king was expected to come with a message of peace. Jesus gave them very little notice to be ready, so they used what was to hand, laying their cloaks on the floor and waving branches from the palm trees in welcome.

The Bible story ends with a question and answer. 'Who can this be?' asked the people of Jerusalem, and the crowd answered, 'This is Jesus, the prophet from Nazareth in Galilee.' Not everyone in the crowd would have grasped exactly how amazing this visitor was, but many realised that Jesus was a prophet, a special messenger from God who would remind them of important truths about God. No doubt, his teaching and news of his miracles would have spread by word of mouth so, as he reached the capital city, people would have been expecting great things from him.

We can look back with all the evidence of the Bible to decide who Jesus is, so we are in a better position than the people of Jerusalem were on that day to answer the question, 'Who can this be?' For Christians, Jesus is more than a prophet. He is the Son of God, their Saviour who forgives their sins and on whose teaching they base their lives. Pause to reflect on the events of Palm Sunday.

Suggestions for songs

- King of kings and Lord of lords (can be sung as a round) (RS 54)
- Hosanna (HON 215)
- All glory, laud and honour (HON 11)
- I'm special (KS 162, TS 222)
- We have a king who rides a donkey (*Someone's Singing, Lord*, A&C Black)
- Hosanna! (*Songs for Every Easter* CD pack, Out of the Ark Music)

Suggested prayer

Thank you, Jesus, that you bring a message of peace to our world. Thank you for reminding us of God's great love for each one of us. Amen

— Easter —

Full of emptiness

Date: Date will vary
Theme: The life of Jesus
Curriculum link: RE

This assembly focuses on the Sunday morning after Jesus died, when some of his closest friends went to visit the tomb where his body had been placed. The assembly can be presented by telling the story below or, as a mark of its importance, by placing each of the suggested visual aids inside a hollow cardboard or plastic Easter egg. These visual aids could be prepared by a selected class in advance and brought to the assembly.

Bible story

Very early on Sunday morning the women went to the tomb, carrying the spices that they had prepared. When they found the stone rolled away from the entrance, they went in. But they did not find the body of the Lord Jesus, and they did not know what to think. Suddenly two men in shining white clothes stood beside them. The women were afraid and bowed to the ground. But the men said, 'Why are you looking in the place of the dead for someone who is alive? Jesus isn't here! He has been raised from death. Remember that while he was still in Galilee, he told you, "The Son of Man will be handed over to sinners who will nail him to a cross. But three days later he will rise to life."' Then they remembered what Jesus had said.

Mary Magdalene, Joanna, Mary the mother of James, and some other women were the ones who had gone to the tomb.

When they returned, they told the eleven apostles and the others what had happened. The apostles thought it was all nonsense, and they would not believe.

But Peter ran to the tomb. And when he stooped down and looked in, he saw only the burial clothes. Then he returned, wondering what had happened.

LUKE 24:1–12

Bible link

Praise God, the Father of our Lord Jesus Christ. God is so good, and by raising Jesus from death, he has given us new life and a hope that lives on.

1 PETER 1:3

Key background information for the teacher

Easter Day is the fulfilment of Jesus' promise that he would die but come back to life on the third day afterwards. The Bible tells us that when Jesus' friends came back to the tomb where his body had been laid, they found it empty except for the pieces of cloth used to wrap the body. The evidence for the resurrection is compelling and would make a worthwhile RE lesson for older children (see page 189 under 'Literacy'). The resurrection is central to Christian belief because Jesus kept his promise and did what no one else had ever done: he came back to life, just as he'd said he would.

Suggestions for visual aids and resources

- A set of six small hollow cardboard or plastic eggs, each large enough to hold one of the following visual aids: small nails, a flower or a small yellow chick (cake decoration), small pebbles, a bandage, a picture of Jesus. The sixth egg should be left empty. (You may wish to mark it in some way, to identify it as the last egg to be opened.)

Ideas for exploring the theme

Prepare the hollow eggs in advance, or ask a class to prepare them, by filling them with items that remind us of Easter. In assembly, invite the children to bring the filled eggs to the front (you could perhaps start with an egg hunt) and take out the items, explaining them as follows.

- The nails remind us that Jesus died by being nailed to a cross.
- The flower (or chick) is a picture of new life and reminds us how Jesus came back to life.
- The pebbles remind us that the body of Jesus was placed in a tomb made of rock, belonging to a local Jewish leader who had met Jesus. A large stone was rolled across the opening and Roman soldiers were ordered to stand guard.
- The bandage reminds us of the pieces of cloth that were used to wrap Jesus' body before it was placed in the rock tomb.
- The picture of Jesus reminds us that, for Christians, Jesus is very important.

Show the children the empty egg. It reminds us that, when Jesus' friends visited the tomb on Sunday morning, it was empty. Jesus had risen to new life.

Suggestions for songs

- This is the day (HON 508)
- Christ the Lord is risen today (HON 80)
- King of kings and Lord of lords (RS 54)
- Easter jubilation (*Songs for Every Easter* CD pack, Out of the Ark)

Suggested prayer

Dear God, thank you that Jesus came back to life to remind us how powerful you are. Thank you that you are a God who keeps promises and can do amazing things. Amen

⊕

Slaying the dragon

Date: 23 April
Theme: Saints of Britain
Curriculum link: History

St George is celebrated as the patron saint of England, although it is quite unlikely that he ever came to Britain. He has probably been adopted as a patron saint because of the legends that grew up around him, which were particularly inspiring for English soldiers fighting in the Crusades. The story of George's fight against the dragon reminds us to be strong in the face of evil and when the things we value are under threat.

Bible story

Finally, let the mighty strength of the Lord make you strong. Put on all the armour that God gives, so you can defend yourself against the devil's tricks. We are not fighting against humans. We are fighting against forces and authorities and against rulers of darkness and powers in the spiritual world. So put on all the armour that God gives. Then when that evil day comes, you will be able to defend yourself. And when the battle is over, you will still be standing firm.

Be ready! Let the truth be like a belt around your waist, and let God's justice protect you like armour. Your desire to tell the good news about peace should be like shoes on your feet. Let your faith be like a shield, and you will be able to stop all the flaming arrows of the evil one. Let God's saving power be like a helmet, and for a sword use God's message that comes from the Spirit.

EPHESIANS 6:10–17

Bible links

I've commanded you to be strong and brave. Don't ever be afraid or discouraged! I am the Lord your God, and I will be there to help you wherever you go.

JOSHUA 1:9

Keep alert. Be firm in your faith. Stay brave and strong. Show love in everything you do.

1 CORINTHIANS 16:13–14

Key background information for the teacher

There is a famous painting of the legend of St George by the 15th-century artist Rogier van der Weyden. It can be found at www.nga.gov/kids/rogier/rogier1.htm. This National Gallery of Art website encourages children to think about how they would paint the story within a landscape of their own place and time period, including a famous monument, just as the original artist did. It also helps them to look for the amazing detail in the original tiny painting. The website tells how dragons were a symbol of evil. By killing this beast, George would be protecting the townspeople from wickedness.

It is likely that George was martyred in Palestine in about AD303. He was born in Cappadocia (Turkey) of Christian parents. He became a Roman soldier and was famous for his bravery, but when he protested against the persecution of Christians in the Roman Empire he was put in prison and tortured. He refused to give up his Christian faith so he was beheaded. England is not the only country to have adopted St George as their patron saint because of his supposed heroics, but he clearly fulfils the English values of bravery and honour.

The story of the dragon probably dates from the twelfth century, long after George's death. Several different versions exist but, in essence, it is a story of how a dragon terrorised a village. When a maiden was offered to the dragon as a sacrifice, St George rode in, rescued the maiden, killed the dragon and saved the day. Many people see this as a story about standing up to what is evil and using everything at our disposal, including God's help.

Suggestions for visual aids and resources

- Picture of a dragon
- Picture of St George (see, for example, the National Gallery of Art website mentioned on page 95, or search the Internet for a 20th-century painting by Wassily Kandinsky; alternatively, Google images of St George)

Ideas for exploring the theme

Explain that you are going to work with the children to tell the famous story of St George. When you mention particular words in the story, the children will respond with an action. Practise the response to the first couple of key words, then add the others, repeating the first two until all have been learnt.

Key words are shown in bold type in the story below.

- **Dragon:** breathe out noisily (as if you are a fire breather)
- **King:** mime putting on a crown, leaving your fingers pointing up to form the zigzag shape
- **Knight(s):** draw your sword from its sheath or salute
- **Sheep:** baa

There was once a **dragon** that lived in a far country, terrorising the people. Whenever the **king** sent his **knights** to fight the **dragon**, it simply breathed fire or flicked its tail, killing them outright. The **dragon** always seemed hungry and the **king** arranged for two **sheep** each day to be fed to it.

It wasn't long before the country ran out of **sheep**, so the **king** decided that a young girl would be given to the **dragon** each day. Each day the girl was chosen by a lottery. One day it was the turn of the **king**'s only daughter. As she was led out to the lair of the **dragon**, the princess and the **king** wept.

Suddenly, a **knight** rode into view on a white horse. He charged straight past the **king** to where the princess was about to be eaten by the **dragon**. George lifted his lance and, as the beast reared up to strike, he struck at the chest of the **dragon** where there were no scales to protect it. The great monster screamed with pain as the lance entered its body and pierced its heart. George had to turn for cover as the **dragon** breathed a final burst of flame towards him. Then all was still.

George had slain the **dragon** and saved the princess. He swept the princess up on to the horse and rode back towards the **king**, who was delighted.

'How did you achieve such a mighty act when all other **knights** had failed?' the **king** asked George.

'I will admit to feeling fear,' the brave **knight** replied, 'but I trusted God to help me defeat this terrible beast.'

'I cannot thank you enough. God did not fail you and you have rescued us from a terrible evil,' announced the **king**.

Show one or more paintings of St George, explaining that the story is used by English people to celebrate their belief that bravery and honour are important characteristics. Christians also look upon the story as a reminder that it is important to ask for God's help when battling against the evil in the world around us—when people or countries bully others or treat them in an unfair or unjust way.

Suggestions for songs

- When a knight won his spurs (CP 50)
- Fight the good fight (HON 128)
- Be bold, be strong (TS 38, KS 17)

Suggested prayer

Dear God, help us to be brave and to fight against evil and injustice whenever we meet it, so that the world we live in may be changed into a fairer place. Amen

— Mark —

Good news about Jesus

Date: 25 April
Theme: Faith in action (Bible disciples)
Curriculum link: Literacy

This assembly focuses on identifying the key events in Jesus' life from the point of view of a biographer. Mark is widely regarded as the first person to have recorded Jesus' life. The assembly highlights the importance of this fact and that Christians rely on such sources to continue to learn about Jesus.

Bible story

Keep on being faithful to what you were taught and to what you believed. After all, you know who taught you these things. Since childhood, you have known the Holy Scriptures that are able to make you wise enough to have faith in Christ Jesus and be saved. Everything in the Scriptures is God's Word. All of it is useful for teaching and helping people and for correcting them and showing them how to live.

2 TIMOTHY 3:14–16

Bible links

This is the good news about Jesus Christ, the Son of God.

MARK 1:1

And after Barnabas and Saul had done the work they were sent to do, they went back to Jerusalem with John, whose other name was Mark.

ACTS 12:25

Mark can be very helpful to me, so please find him and bring him with you.

2 TIMOTHY 4:11

Key background information for the teacher

The Gospel writer Mark, although not one of the original twelve disciples, clearly knew Jesus well. It is assumed that Mark was younger than the other disciples but travelled widely with Jesus and then with Peter (to Rome) and Paul (to Cyprus). He would therefore have seen the gospel message being shared not only by Jesus but also by two of the greatest evangelists of his generation. Both Peter and Paul claimed that Mark was like a son to them, and he was Barnabas' cousin. Barnabas also travelled widely with Paul (see pages 136–137). It is believed by many that Mark was the young man who ran away naked when Jesus was arrested (see Mark 14:51–52). It is thought that he died for his faith in AD68 in Alexandria, where he was sharing his beliefs.

Whereas both Matthew and Luke had a specific audience in mind when they wrote their Gospels, it is not clear who Mark was writing for. It has been suggested that he wrote his Gospel for those living in the Roman Empire at the time who did not understand how the Jewish people lived. Perhaps he simply realised that it was important to record the key events of Jesus' life and his teachings, and knew that future generations would rely on this evidence.

The first half of Mark's Gospel is set mostly in Galilee and the second half in or near Jerusalem. Like all biographers, he would have had to select what he considered to be the most important information. As John wrote at the end of his Gospel, 'Jesus did many other things. If they were all written in books, I don't suppose there would be room enough in the whole world for all the books' (John 21:25).

There is little doubt about the reliability of what Mark wrote about Jesus because it was recorded within the lifetime of the earliest believers, who would have been able to correct him if he had made mistakes. In fact, it is believed that Matthew and Luke both relied heavily on Mark's Gospel when writing their own.

Suggestions for visual aids and resources

• A mixture of biographies and autobiographies of famous people

Ideas for exploring the theme

Show the children the books you have collected and establish that they are all about people and their lives. Some of these people may still be alive and others may have died. Ask if anyone can tell you the 'genre' of these types of books. Establish the difference between a biography and an autobiography, which is that a biographer writes about someone else while an autobiographer writes about their own life.

Ask the children what they would include in a biography of someone famous, and then apply their answers to Jesus, explaining that Mark wrote the earliest known biography of Jesus. Go on to look at some of the important things about Jesus that Mark would have wanted to include, such as his teaching, his miracles, events in his life, his friends (and enemies) and his achievements—what he would have been remembered for by the people who knew him. Explain that, surprisingly, Mark omits the story of Jesus' birth, beginning instead with his baptism. He does, however, record the important news of Jesus' death and resurrection.

Ask the children why they think people write about the lives of others. Ask why they think it is important to have an accurate biography of Jesus and who might want to read it.

Thousands of people have learnt about Jesus by reading the biblical accounts. These accounts are very important as Christians believe that they contain the words and teaching of Jesus as well as details about his life. Without these writings, it would be difficult to understand how important Jesus is or why so many people have based their lives on him.

Explain that Mark's account of Jesus' life was used by Matthew and Luke when they came to write their Gospels. They also added new information of their own, including stories about Jesus' birth and different stories of his appearances after he came back to life, each with a particular audience in mind.

Suggestions for songs

- Spirit of God (CP 63)
- Come my brothers, praise the Lord (CP 20)
- Go, tell it on the mountain (CP 24)

Suggested prayer

Thank you for Mark, who wrote down what he knew about Jesus. Help us to remember how special the Bible is and how many people still use it today as a guidebook for life. Amen

⊕

— Florence Nightingale —

The lady with the lamp
(and a scrubbing brush!)

Date: 12 May
Theme: Faith in action (later disciples)
Curriculum link: History

Florence Nightingale put her faith into action in a quite dramatic
way, using her skills and training for the benefit of people in need.

Bible story

'Teacher, what is the most important commandment in the
Law?' Jesus answered: Love the Lord your God with all your
heart, soul, and mind. This is the first and most important
commandment. The second most important commandment
is like this one. And it is, 'Love others as much as you love
yourself.' All the Law of Moses and the Books of the Prophets
are based on these two commandments.
MATTHEW 22:36–40

Bible link

Make your light shine, so that others will see the good that you
do and will praise your Father in heaven.
MATTHEW 5:16

Key background information for the teacher

Florence Nightingale was born on 12 May 1820. She grew up at the same time as the girl destined to become Queen Victoria. Florence was from a wealthy family but wasn't content to learn to be a lady and run a household, as was customary. She was clearly determined and sensed that God had a different role for her to play, something important to achieve for him. It is unclear whether she felt that this calling was specifically to care for those who were unwell but she decided to train as a nurse. She ended up knowing so much about keeping healthy and how hospitals worked that Members of Parliament would ask her questions.

When war broke out in the Crimea (then part of the Russian Empire), Florence asked to go with a team of nurses to look after wounded soldiers. On her arrival in Scutari (in modern Turkey), she was disgusted by the conditions in which the soldiers were kept, not least because they already had so-called nurses looking after them. The wounded men were lying on straw, with rats and fleas bothering them, and they were being kept too close to others, so diseases could easily spread.

Florence knew that the men wouldn't get better if she didn't use the skills she had learnt in London, and the first thing she ordered was 200 scrubbing brushes! Her team of nurses cleaned the place up and looked after the soldiers using the skills they had learnt at home. Many of the men got better when the conditions improved.

Florence was very strict with the other nurses and would check that they were doing their job well. At night she would walk round with a lamp to see if all her instructions were being carried out. Because of this she became known as 'the lady with the lamp'.

Florence Nightingale is widely recognised as the founder of training for nurses, having helped to found a training school at St Thomas' Hospital in London, which is still a teaching hospital, used to train both nurses and doctors.

Suggestions for visual aids and resources

- A scrubbing brush and bucket

Ideas for exploring the theme

Show the children the scrubbing brush and bucket and ask them who they think would use these items as part of their job. Say that the answer in today's assembly takes us back to Victorian times. Any more guesses?

Explain that today we will be thinking about a famous Christian who put what she believed into action—Florence Nightingale. What was she famous for?

Florence Nightingale had set out not really sure what God wanted her to do but knowing that it wouldn't be a quiet life at home as a wealthy lady. She learned as much as she could, trained hard and, when she saw a need, got on and used what she had learnt. With her firm determination and training, she ended up not just changing the lives of a few soldiers but also changing the whole way that nurses trained and worked.

She is a really good example of someone who wanted to make a difference, helping others and doing her best for God and the people she met.

Suggestions for songs

- Jesus' hands were kind hands (JP 134, KS 194)
- Make me a channel of your peace (OSS 81, JP 161, HON 328)

Suggested prayer

Thank you for nurses who look after us when we need to go to hospital. Thank you for Florence Nightingale, who invented proper training for nurses so that they now learn how to do the job well. Thank you for all the people who work in hospitals, looking after people who are unwell and keeping everything clean and hygienic. Amen

⊕

A family with a message

Date: 24 May
Theme: Faith in action (later disciples)
Curriculum link: Music

What a family the Wesleys were! Across several generations, some became fine evangelists and teachers, others had strong organisational gifts and yet others had a real flair for composing music and lyrics. This assembly looks at the lives of brothers John and Charles Wesley as an example of those who have tried to keep the Christian message fresh and relevant and those who write music and lyrics for us to use in school and church.

Bible story

Let the message about Christ completely fill your lives, while you use all your wisdom to teach and instruct each other. With thankful hearts, sing psalms, hymns, and spiritual songs to God. Whatever you say or do should be done in the name of the Lord Jesus, as you give thanks to God the Father because of him.
COLOSSIANS 3:16–17

Bible link

When you meet together, sing psalms, hymns, and spiritual songs, as you praise the Lord with all your heart. Always use the name of our Lord Jesus Christ to thank God the Father for everything.
EPHESIANS 5:19–20

Key background information for the teacher

A movement known as the Methodist revival began within the Church of England in the 18th century. It was started by a group of men who were all students at Oxford, including John Wesley and his younger brother Charles. They focused on Bible study and a methodical approach to both the Bible and Christian living. The term 'Methodist' was a college nickname that was given to them. They met with each other every week, fasting regularly and refusing luxuries and most forms of amusement. They often visited people who were in poverty or unwell as well as prisoners in jail.

The Methodists felt that the Church of England had become apathetic and out of touch with the need for Christians to act in a disciplined way. Wherever they went, they encouraged people to be more serious about their faith and to consider how to apply it. They were well known for preaching wherever they could find an audience, including in the open air, at a time when it was considered odd to preach outside a church building. Traditional church leaders naturally saw their enthusiasm as challenging and accused them of fanaticism.

It is clear from their writings, hymns and preaching that the Methodists believed that each person should be challenged to make a personal expression of their belief that salvation is received through trusting Jesus as Saviour and Lord, and that Christians should both ask for and expect the Holy Spirit to help them live in a way that pleases God. Nowadays we would say that they belong to the wing of the church family called 'evangelical', because of their commitment to individual salvation, regular personal Bible study and openness to the work of the Holy Spirit.

Members of the Church of England and the Methodist Church often work closely together today and there have been high-level church committees discussing a merger. Many local Christians from both groups share buildings and worship together.

Suggestions for visual aids and resources

- Two signs, one with the words 'Church of England' written on it and the other with the word 'Methodist'

Ideas for exploring the theme

Have a mini competition to vote for the most popular song sung at assembly. Alternatively, prepare a list of popular songs in advance and announce the result at the assembly. If appropriate, ask the children to say briefly why they like that particular song.

Make the point that, for hundreds of years, people with gifts in music and poetry have written new songs for us to enjoy. Sometimes old songs have been given new words. The idea is to make it fun for us to worship God and to learn from the words about the story of God in the Bible.

Explain that every generation of Christians has had its favourite composers and song writers. Some of these composers wrote their own tunes, while others borrowed them from classical music or from folk tunes. The word 'carol', which we associate with Christmas, originally meant a French folk dance: lively dance tunes were borrowed to sing at Christmas celebrations. Today, folk tunes are still often used in worship: for example, the Iona Community in Scotland has been very successfully writing new words to Scottish folk tunes.

Back in the 1800s, two brothers, whose father was a vicar in the Church of England, both went to study at Oxford before becoming ministers themselves. They felt that church services were getting rather boring and that many ministers weren't excited enough about telling everyone the good news of Jesus. Not enough people, in their view, knew the stories in the Bible, prayed regularly and understood about the love and forgiveness that Jesus offered them.

The brothers, John and Charles Wesley, set off around the country, preaching about Jesus. If they weren't allowed into the churches, they stood outside, wherever there was a large space, and people came to listen to them. Many people became Christians as a result. Not surprisingly, many Church of England ministers felt annoyed, and eventually these new groups of Christians who wanted to study the Bible and worship in a lively way had to meet away from the main church. They were known as Methodists. Many Methodist churches exist today and work happily alongside the nearby churches, sometimes sharing a building or joining together for services.

Charles Wesley had a particular gift for writing hymn lyrics. Some of his most famous are still used today, such as 'Love divine, all loves excelling', which is often sung at weddings, and 'Hark! the herald-angels sing', which is sung at Christmas.

Today, new hymns and songs are still being written for worship. If you have used any of the *Out of the Ark* CDs or songs by current writers, you could use one now to close the assembly.

Suggestions for songs

- Shine, Jesus, shine (HON 317)
- I'm special (JP 106, TS 222, KS 162)
- This child (TS 511)

Suggested prayer

Dear God, thank you for the people who have written hymns and songs for us to use in our assemblies. Thank you for the gift of music and for giving us voices to sing your praise. Amen

⊕

— Bede —

Words, work and worship

Date: 25 May
Theme: Saints of Britain (later disciples)
Curriculum links: History, Literacy

The intention of this assembly is to give children a flavour of life in a medieval monastery in eighth-century England and to remind them, through looking at the life of Bede, that Christians have always valued the opportunity to study the Bible, pray and worship. From the age of seven, Bede lived in the monastery at Wearmouth and Jarrow in Northumbria, with very occasional visits to places nearby. He is quoted as being very happy with this life: 'I have devoted my energies to a study of the Scriptures, observing monastic discipline, and singing the daily services in church. Study, teaching, and writing have always been my delight.'

Bible story

Your word is a lamp that gives light wherever I walk.
PSALM 119:105

Bible link

It is wonderful to be grateful and to sing your praises, Lord Most High! It is wonderful each morning to tell about your love and at night to announce how faithful you are.
PSALM 92:1–2

Key background information for the teacher

Irish monks from monasteries established by St Patrick spread Christianity into Cornwall, Wales and Scotland. Monasteries were also founded at Lindisfarne by St Aidan, Iona by St Columba and Whithorn (in Scotland) by St Ninian. These monks spent much of their time alone but met together also in a chapel.

A big change took place in AD597, when the 'Benedictine Rule' was established by St Augustine as a pattern for monastic life, with monks living, praying and working as a community. There were six main orders of monks established in Britain over the following thousand years, which varied in the strictness with which they applied Benedictine principles. Generally speaking, life for a monk was made up of hard physical work, prayer and study, although some orders encouraged the employment of 'lay brothers', who did much of the physical work to enable the monks to concentrate on learning and praying.

A day in an abbey or monastery was regulated by regular prayer services, every three hours, day and night. In between the services, monks would sleep or work on ways of sustaining the community. Their work might involve growing food, extending the buildings, raising sheep or looking after pilgrims who came to worship at the relics or bones of a saint. Copying out manuscripts was also a key role, as monks were among the only educated members of society in the medieval world.

Beautifully illustrated manuscripts were a strong feature of Celtic Christianity, and the world-famous Lindisfarne Gospels are on view today in the British Museum in London. By the time Henry VIII split the church from the control of Rome in the 1530s, there were about 500 different religious houses for men or women. After this point, the combination of the Black Death and the programme of dissolution organised by Henry brought about a collapse of the system. The churches that survived tended to be those in well-populated areas. Some of the best abbeys remaining in Britain today with monastic links are Fountains, Glastonbury, Rievaulx and Tintern (all ruins) and Westminster Abbey, Bath Abbey and Durham Cathedral, which are all very much active today.

Suggestions for visual aids and resources

- A poster saying 'welcome' in different languages (optional)
- A picture of a monk from the medieval period
- Three cards with the words 'words', 'work' and 'worship' written on them
- An illuminated letter design from a medieval manuscript

Ideas for exploring the theme

Show the 'welcome' poster if available, and ask the children if they can say 'hello' in a different language. This language might reflect their own home background or holidays they have taken. Move on to think of the languages spoken by different races that have invaded Britain down the years—Roman, Saxon, Viking, Norman and so on.

Explain that today you are going to look at the life of a monk who lived in a monastery in England in the eighth century. His name was Bede and he lived in the north-east of England, near today's city of Newcastle. In Bede's time, the headquarters of the church was in Rome, so the main language used in the church was Latin.

In those days, much of people's time would be spent growing food and looking after animals, maintaining shelters and collecting firewood with which to cook and keep warm. The monks would spend their days working, studying and praying (show the three cards). It is likely that monks such as Bede, who had a fine mind, would have been encouraged to do more studying and less of the hard physical work of farming. The monks were also committed to attending eight services of prayer and worship each day at roughly three-hourly intervals, starting at two o'clock in the morning, as well as some study. Some of the most important objects that survive from this period are amazing abbey buildings and beautiful copies of parts of the Bible that the monks wrote out by hand.

Bede was the first person, as far as we know, to write important books in the English language. He wrote a lot in Latin, as all monks learned to do, but he also translated John's Gospel into Old English, a job that he finished just before he died. His most famous work is *A History of the English Church and People*, which is still in print today, giving us a history up to the year AD729. Just as we are trained to do at school, Bede separated what he thought was fact from hearsay or opinion, and recorded the sources of his information. His literacy teacher would have been very pleased with him if he was at school today! He also wrote books on grammar and astronomy as well as hymns and poetry.

Suggestions for songs

- Spirit of God (CP 63)
- For all the saints (HON 134)

Suggested prayer

Dear God, help us to value the Bible as a special book that we can learn from, just as Bede did. Thank you for people who study it so that they can explain it to us better. Thank you for all the Christians who have based their lives on the teaching of Jesus and made such a difference to the world. Amen

— Ascension Day —

Time to go!

Date: Date will vary
Theme: The life of Jesus
Curriculum link: Drama

This assembly gives an overview of Jesus' life but focuses on his final moments before his ascension—the time when he returned to heaven to be with his Father.

Bible story

Jesus led his disciples out to Bethany, where he raised his hands and blessed them. As he was doing this, he left and was taken up to heaven. After his disciples had worshipped him, they returned to Jerusalem and were very happy. They spent their time in the temple, praising God.

LUKE 24:50–53

Bible link

While Jesus' disciples were talking about what had happened, Jesus appeared and greeted them. They were frightened and terrified because they thought they were seeing a ghost. But Jesus said, 'Why are you so frightened? Why do you doubt? Look at my hands and my feet and see who I am! Touch me and find out for yourselves. Ghosts don't have flesh and bones as you see I have.' After Jesus said this, he showed them his hands and his feet. The disciples were so glad and amazed that they could not believe it. Jesus then asked them, 'Do you have something to eat?' They gave him a piece of baked fish. He took it and ate it as they watched.

Jesus said to them, 'While I was still with you, I told you that everything written about me in the Law of Moses, the Books of the Prophets, and in the Psalms had to happen.' Then he helped them understand the Scriptures. He told them:

The Scriptures say that the Messiah must suffer, then three days later he will rise from death. They also say that all people of every nation must be told in my name to turn to God, in order to be forgiven. So beginning in Jerusalem, you must tell everything that has happened. I will send you the one my Father has promised, but you must stay in the city until you are given power from heaven.

LUKE 24:36–49

Key background information for the teacher

Jesus appeared to his disciples many times after the resurrection. When the time came for him to return to heaven, he made it clear that there would be no further appearances. This meant that the Spirit he had promised would take over his presence with the disciples, coming to equip his followers with the knowledge and power they would need to continue his work. This is hinted at when the assembly concludes but is the main subject of the Pentecost theme.

Suggestions for visual aids and resources

- A selection of objects or pictures that link to key parts of Jesus' life, for example:
  - ❖ Birth: a doll wrapped in a small blanket, ornamental angel, toy donkey, figures to represent Mary and Joseph, a toy stable
  - ❖ Ministry: sandals to represent travelling, Bible, bread to link with miracles

- ❖ Death: a wooden cross and a palm cross
- ❖ Resurrection: picture of a grave with the stone rolled back
- ❖ Ascension: cloud shape, a cardboard crown
- Photocopies of the script on pages 117–119

Ideas for exploring the theme

Explain that you are going to show some objects and pictures and want the children to give you ideas as to how they fit into the story of Jesus' life.

Show the different objects and pictures and talk about which part of Jesus' life they represent. Conclude with the images associated with the ascension and talk about the time when Jesus had to go back to his Father in heaven. Introduce the idea of saying goodbye and talk about ways in which people say goodbye. You might talk about the words we use, or prearrange for children to act out very short scenes, such as a dad dropping his child off at school, two friends saying goodbye after school, or someone who is moving house but wants to stay in touch with their friends.

Point out that words for 'goodbye' have different meanings in some languages. For example, in French, *adieu* has a finality about it, whereas *au revoir* means 'until we see you again' and *a bientôt* expects the next meeting to be soon. Other languages also pick up the idea of 'until the next time': the German *auf Wiedersehen* has this meaning. When Jesus finally left his disciples to return to his heavenly Father, he didn't expect to see his disciples again on earth, but he had promised to come back to them through his Holy Spirit.

The Bible records much of Jesus' teaching before the final moment of the ascension, but doesn't record his actual words when saying goodbye. Quite how he disappeared, no one quite knows. Some people think he was 'taken up' into heaven by God, while others believe that a cloud came down and covered him, and when it had lifted he was gone. It's very mysterious.

Refer back to the last one or two objects or pictures. The cloud reminds us of the way Jesus went up into heaven, and the crown reminds how Christians believe that Jesus returned to be king in heaven, sitting alongside his Father.

Is this the end of the story? There is more to read in the Bible about what happened to Jesus' friends once he had gone. Say that if we think about God in three main ways as Father, Son and Holy Spirit, there's quite a bit more to hear about. Some of Jesus' friends may have felt sad about saying goodbye, but they were in for a big surprise when his Holy Spirit arrived. Then they realised that the Spirit was God's power for everyone who wants to follow Jesus… but that's another story.

Finish with the following puppet sketch, which is designed for a narrator and two puppets. In the script, Charlie Crocodile is a strong character who is full of mischief. Lily Lamb has a softer side and is upset. However, any two puppets could be used, or children could be encouraged to make their own puppets as a project. By using a simple puppet theatre shape or clothes horse, the puppeteers will be able to pin their scripts out of sight of the audience, but they will need to use very big voices to be heard.

— Cast —

Narrator
Lily Lamb
Charlie Crocodile

Lily appears: she is crying.

Narrator: What on earth is the matter? Why are you so upset?
Lily: I've just said goodbye to my friend Ellie. I might never see her again.
Narrator: Oh dear.

Charlie:	*(Appears cheerfully, not noticing that Lily is upset)* Hello, everyone!
Narrator:	Oh, hello, Charlie. I've just been talking to Lily about her friend Ellie going away.
Charlie:	Yes, it's always sad when that happens, but it's not always the end of the story, is it?
Narrator:	What do you mean?
Charlie:	Well, you can keep in touch.
Lily:	But she's moving to the other side of the world.
Narrator:	*(To audience)* How do you think Lily can keep in touch with her friend now she'll be so far away?
Charlie:	You could write her a letter. Then of course there's email. I often email my friends in America and here as well. It's much cheaper than phoning, but I do that sometimes too as a treat, like at Christmas!
Narrator:	Do you know the story of Jesus' ascension? *(Say the word 'ascension' as if sneezing)*
Lily:	Bless you!
Narrator:	Pardon?
Lily:	I thought you sneezed. You said 'a-shoshun'.
Narrator:	Oh, right. No, I said 'ascension'.
Charlie:	What does that mean?
Narrator:	It's when Jesus went back to heaven to be with his Father.
Lily:	How did that happen? Did he beam up, like on *Star Trek*?
Narrator:	No, I don't think so, but nobody really knows.
Charlie:	*(Excitedly)* Perhaps he went in a rocket!
Narrator:	Well, rockets hadn't been invented then, so that wouldn't have been right either. The Bible says that

he was taken out of sight but doesn't explain how. His friends just stood there looking at the sky in amazement.

Charlie: They must have really missed him!

Narrator: Yes, of course they did, but he did promise to stay in touch. A bit like your friend really, Lily. Remember, you can keep in touch with her by phone or email.

Lily: OK. I'm still a bit sad but I will try to stay in touch.

Charlie: Can we email Jesus or phone him up?

Narrator: Not exactly, but it's easier than that. No need for broadband or even dial-up connections. The Bible says that when people believe in Jesus, they can talk to him when they pray.

Lily: Can we do that now?

Charlie: What, pray?

Lily: Yes.

Narrator: Of course we can. Let's get still and concentrate. *(To audience)* If you would like to join in, you can say 'Amen' at the end of the prayer.

Suggestions for songs

- Crown him with many crowns (HON 103)
- The head that once was crowned with thorns (HON 480)
- King of kings and Lord of lords (RS 54)
- Lord of the dance (CP 22)

Suggested prayer

Dear God, thank you that we can find out all about Jesus' life in the Bible. Thank you that the Bible tells us that Jesus will listen to us when we pray. Help us to listen to the needs of others, too, and to follow Jesus' example of loving other people every day. Amen

⊕

Worth waiting for!

Date: Date will vary
Theme: Special days and celebrations
Curriculum link: Literacy

This assembly is a retelling of the events of Pentecost, using exclamation marks as a way of highlighting key ideas. It must have been an amazing day in terms of its sights and sounds, and the transformation of Jesus' followers would have been exciting as they sensed the new possibilities that were brought about by being filled with the power of God's Spirit.

Bible story

On the day of Pentecost all the Lord's followers were together in one place. Suddenly there was a noise from heaven like the sound of a mighty **wind**! It filled the house where they were meeting. Then they saw what looked like fiery **tongues** moving in all directions, and a **tongue** came and settled on each person there. The **Holy Spirit** took control of everyone, and they began speaking whatever **languages** the Spirit let them speak.

Many religious Jews from every country in the world were living in Jerusalem. And when they heard this noise, a crowd gathered. But they were surprised, because they were hearing everything in their own **languages**. They were excited and amazed, and said:

Don't all these who are speaking come from Galilee? Then why do we hear them speaking our very own **languages**? … We all hear them using our own **languages** to tell the wonderful things God has done.

Everyone was excited and confused. Some of them even kept asking each other, 'What does all this mean?' Others made fun of the Lord's followers and said, 'They are drunk.'

Peter stood with the eleven apostles and spoke in a loud and clear voice to the crowd:

Friends and everyone else living in Jerusalem, listen carefully to what I have to say! You are wrong to think that these people are drunk. After all, it is only nine o'clock in the morning…'

Peter said, 'Turn back to God! Be baptised in the name of Jesus Christ, so that your sins will be forgiven. Then you will be given the **Holy Spirit**. This promise is for you and your children. It is for everyone our Lord God will choose, no matter where they live.'

Peter told them many other things as well. Then he said, 'I beg you to save yourselves from what will happen to all these evil people.' On that day about three thousand believed his message and were baptised.

ACTS 2:1–8, 11b–15, 38–41

Bible link

While [Jesus] was still with them, he said: Don't leave Jerusalem yet. Wait here for the Father to give you the Holy Spirit, just as I told you he has promised to do. John baptised with water, but in a few days you will be baptised with the Holy Spirit.

ACTS 1:4–5

Key background information for the teacher

Pentecost was a Jewish festival that took place 50 days after Passover. For Christians, it is celebrated 50 days after Jesus ate his last supper with his disciples, which was a Passover meal, so Pentecost falls six weeks after Easter. It is celebrated in particular because it marks the day when the Holy Spirit came upon the rather despondent and puzzled disciples, giving them the skill, boldness and power to spread the gospel message about Jesus. This event took place in

Jerusalem at a time when it was full of pilgrims from many parts of the country and beyond. Each person listening to Peter's message appeared to hear it in his or her own language. Therefore, the message took on a global significance as the people who responded carried the news back to their own towns.

So many people (about 3000 in total) believed the gospel message on this occasion that Pentecost is often called the birthday of the Church.

Suggestions for visual aids and resources

- The following punctuation marks on cards for children to hold:
  - ❖ Exclamation mark
  - ❖ Speech marks
  - ❖ Question mark
  - ❖ Colon
  - ❖ Full stop
  - ❖ Ellipsis
- A hair dryer (and extension lead if needed)

Ideas for exploring the theme

Retell the narrative of Pentecost, using the Bible story printed on pages 120–121. Ask the children to respond in the following ways to the key words (shown in bold in the Bible story):

- **Wind:** one long blow
- **Tongue(s):** flickering hands
- **Holy Spirit:** either or both of the above
- **Languages:** say 'hello' in English or another language if possible

Next, use the punctuation mark cards to highlight key parts of the story. This could be done as a question-and-answer session. For example:

- **Exclamation mark:** The disciples were waiting in Jerusalem. What were they waiting for? The Holy Spirit, as promised by Jesus. When the Spirit came, it was a massive surprise, more exciting and powerful than they could have imagined.
- **Speech marks:** As the disciples were filled with the Holy Spirit, who did they want to tell people about? Jesus, of course. Amazingly, all the people in the city heard the disciples' message in their own languages. Who got up and gave a speech, using his knowledge of the Bible and of Jesus? Peter.
- **Question mark:** People naturally had questions to ask. What were those questions? 'How can we hear them in our own language? What does this mean? Are these men drunk? What's going on?'
- **Colon:** Peter used the opportunity to get up and list many of God's amazing actions. He explained everything that had happened to Jesus as part of God's great plan, linking Jesus back to his ancestor King David. In particular, he was keen to speak of the death and resurrection of Jesus, as well as the promised coming of the Holy Spirit. (Explain that you didn't read the whole chapter from the Bible as it would have taken more time than was available.)
- **Full stop:** When do we use a full stop? Peter's message was that people should stop what they were doing and change the way they were living. People should make a fresh start and live in the way that Jesus taught.
- **Ellipsis:** An ellipsis shows that the message has been interrupted or is continuing. Watch this space! There were plenty more adventures to come as the gospel message spread.

Explain that, for Jesus' friends, carrying on without him was like having no energy, a bit like having a hair dryer but not plugging it in. (Show the hair dryer.) On the day of Pentecost, there was a massive burst of power from God to start a whole new stage of his story—the spreading of the good news about Jesus. Before this, the disciples had been waiting and feeling rather sad, puzzled, disappointed and perhaps scared. Now they had energy and skill from God to remember the words of Jesus and to share them with everybody. (Plug the hair dryer in and turn it on.)

Suggestions for songs

- Jesus is Lord (HON 270)
- He's got the whole world (CP 19)
- Father, we adore you (HON 125)
- Go tell it on the mountain (CP 24)

Suggested prayer

Dear God, whenever we feel fed up and sad, help us to remember that you can come and be with us in a fresh way. Thank you for the first disciples who allowed the Holy Spirit to help them and use them. Help us to be willing to be a part of your great plan to change the world. Help us to remember Jesus' words and to live fruitful lives. Amen

— Trinity —

Three in one and one in three

Date: Date will vary
Theme: Special days and celebrations
Curriculum links: Design Technology, Literacy, Maths

What is God like? It's quite a tall order to answer that question in a few words, but one way Christians might explain it is in terms of the Trinity—the three key states in which God exists. It is a mystery that something can be three and one at the same time, but this is how Christians view God because of how they experience him and the way he is presented in the Bible. God is seen as Father, Son and Holy Spirit. It would be impossible for children to grasp the concept of the Trinity in a few short minutes. In fact, it is probably more than a lifetime's work to gain much understanding of this complex idea, so it's best to view this assembly as a simple presentation of what Christians believe and will spend their lives trying to understand better.

Bible story

I have told you these things while I am still with you. But the Holy Spirit will come and help you, because the Father will send the Spirit to take my place. The Spirit will teach you everything and will remind you of what I said while I was with you.

JOHN 14:25–26

Bible links

In the beginning God created the heavens and the earth. The earth was barren, with no form of life; it was under a roaring ocean covered with darkness. But the Spirit of God was moving over the water.

GENESIS 1:1–2

As soon as Jesus came out of the water, he saw the sky open and the Holy Spirit coming down to him like a dove. A voice from heaven said, 'You are my own dear Son, and I am pleased with you.'

MARK 1:10–11

I have been given all authority in heaven and on earth! Go to the people of all nations and make them my disciples. Baptise them in the name of the Father, the Son, and the Holy Spirit, and teach them to do everything I have told you. I will be with you always, even until the end of the world.

MATTHEW 28:18–20

God loved the people of this world so much that he gave his only Son, so that everyone who has faith in him will have eternal life and never really die. God did not send his Son into the world to condemn its people. He sent him to save them!

JOHN 3:16–17

Key background information for the teacher

Trinity Sunday is celebrated a week after Pentecost. This is an opportunity for Christians to remind themselves of the nature of God as revealed in the Bible, and follows on naturally from the celebration of the coming of the Holy Spirit, with its outpouring of God's power.

All the models and images we use to explain the Trinity are bound to be limited. Part of the journey of faith is to discover more and more about God. Being a Christian is about being in a relationship with God, so, as in any relationship, it is natural to learn more as we get to know him better. Trinity Sunday gives Christians a chance to think about the nature of God and to marvel at it. There are many references in the Bible that show the Father, the Son and the Holy Spirit, all interlinked in the nature of God.

Suggestions for visual aids and resources

- The prefix 'Tri' and the word 'Unity' on two cards that can be overlapped to form the word 'Trinity'
- A large triangle with 'Father', 'Son' and 'Holy Spirit' written, one word in each corner
- A Celtic overlap of three circles, forming a 'triangle' in the centre
- Sticky tack or paperclips

Ideas for exploring the theme

Show the two cards and ask the children about their knowledge of the suffixes 'tri' and 'uni'. Give them one minute to discuss with a neighbour or do a 'think, pair, share' exercise, stopping the discussion at an agreed signal. Collect responses and agree with the children that 'tri' means 'three' and 'uni' means 'one'.

Ask the children if they can think of something that can be both one thing and three things at the same time, or something that has just three parts or states (such as an egg or water). Explain that this idea is important to Christians because it helps them to understand what God is like. Overlap the two cards to form the word 'Trinity' and explain that Christians use this word to remind them that God is Father, Son and Holy Spirit.

Another way that might help us to understand this idea a little more is to think of a three-part shape. Show the Celtic overlapping circles. Imagine that each circle is one part of the Trinity. Whenever we look at one circle, we are aware that it is part of a three-sided shape. In the same way, when we learn about one person of the Trinity, it is linked to learning more about the other two persons. Read John 14:25–26 (printed on page 125) to demonstrate this idea.

Show the children what a strong shape the triangle is. Any two of the sides hold the third one firmly in place. (Some of them may have learned about this when looking at structures such as the Eiffel Tower, roofing rafters, electricity pylons, and so on, which use triangular shapes in their design.) Show the children how, when three circles are overlapped equally, a three-way loop is formed with a rounded triangle in the middle.

Finish by saying that, for Christians, learning what God is like helps them to understand God a little better, not only as the Creator of the world but also as God's Son, Jesus, and the Holy Spirit who helps them in their daily lives.

Suggestions for songs

- He's got the whole world (CP 19)
- Father, we adore you (HON 125)

Suggested prayer

O God, you are too wonderful for us to understand what you are really like. Thank you that the Bible tells us how you have shown yourself as the Creator of the world, as Jesus and as the Holy Spirit. Help us, as we journey through life, to learn more and more about you and your amazing love for each one of us. Amen

— Boniface —

Timber!

Date: 5 June
Theme: Saints of Britain (later disciples)
Curriculum links: History, Geography

The stories of many saints are based on legends that have grown up alongside one or two factual incidents of particular significance in their lives. The story of the tree that Boniface cut down is used to illustrate his bravery in countering the superstition of the Saxons. His commitment and willingness to share the gospel message among people who were regarded as hostile is an example of perseverance.

Bible story

Then Elijah continued: I am the Lord's only prophet, but Baal has four hundred and fifty prophets. Bring us two bulls. Baal's prophets can take one of them, kill it, and cut it into pieces. Then they can put the meat on the wood without lighting the fire. I will do the same thing with the other bull, and I won't light a fire under it either. The prophets of Baal will pray to their god, and I will pray to the Lord. The one who answers by starting the fire is God.

'That's a good idea,' everyone agreed. Elijah said to Baal's prophets, 'There are more of you, so you go first. Pick out a bull and get it ready, but don't light the fire. Then pray to your god.' They chose their bull, then they got it ready and prayed to Baal all morning, asking him to start the fire. They danced around the altar and shouted, 'Answer us, Baal!' But there was no answer.

At midday, Elijah began making fun of them. 'Pray louder!' he said. 'Baal must be a god. Maybe he's daydreaming or using the toilet or travelling somewhere. Or perhaps he's asleep, and you have to wake him up.' ...

When it was time for the evening sacrifice, Elijah prayed: Our Lord, you are the God of Abraham, Isaac, and Israel. Now, prove that you are the God of this nation, and that I, your servant, have done this at your command. Please answer me, so these people will know that you are the Lord God, and that you will turn their hearts back to you.

The Lord immediately sent fire, and it burnt up the sacrifice, the wood, and the stones. It scorched the ground everywhere around the altar and dried up every drop of water in the ditch. When the crowd saw what had happened, they all bowed down and shouted, 'The Lord is God! The Lord is God!'

1 KINGS 18:22–27, 36–39

Bible links

I run towards the goal, so that I can win the prize of being called to heaven. This is the prize that God offers because of what Christ Jesus has done.

PHILIPPIANS 3:14

Jesus came to them and said: I have been given all authority in heaven and on earth! Go to the people of all nations and make them my disciples. Baptise them in the name of the Father, the Son, and the Holy Spirit, and teach them to do everything I have told you. I will be with you always, even until the end of the world.

MATTHEW 28:18–20

Key background information for the teacher

Boniface was a Saxon born to a wealthy family in Crediton, Devon, around AD670–680. At the time, that area of the country was called Wessex. He was called Wynfrith at birth but was given the name Boniface by the Pope later in his life.

Boniface was a Christian and wanted to share his faith. He knew that although many people in Britain had heard about Jesus, the Saxons came from a region of Europe where there were few believers. He spoke their language but knew that they were a tough lot. After all, many of them had invaded and taken control of Britain!

Boniface's first visit to Frisia (which extended from the north-western Netherlands through north-west Germany to the border of Denmark) was a failure. No one wanted to listen to him and the king wouldn't meet him. The three friends who accompanied him on his journey must have wondered if they'd made the right decision, but Boniface didn't give up easily. He still felt that it was important to share the beliefs that were so much a part of his life. He really believed that the Frisians were missing out on good news. He went back to England and spent two years in preparation to return.

His second trip didn't go well at first. Boniface decided that he needed to build a church building out of wood, so he went off to chop down some trees. When he tried to fell one particular tree, people shouted at him because it was a tree sacred to their god, Thor, the god of lightning. They expected him to be struck by lightning, but Boniface trusted God and chopped down the tree. Nothing happened, and he used the incident as an excuse to talk to the people about the God who created the whole world and sent his Son, Jesus, to share his love. Many people who saw what Boniface did and heard his words became Christians. This gave him confidence to continue travelling around, sharing his faith in Jesus. So it was that a Christian from England became the patron saint of Germany and the Netherlands. He was, in fact, England's patron saint for 300 years, before being replaced by St George. Boniface died on 5 June 754, so this has become his special day.

Boniface trained at the monasteries in Exeter and Southampton, then became a priest and later became a bishop. After his initial attempt to evangelise Frisia failed, he asked the Pope's blessing on his next visit. He set off for Rome, and then on to mainland Europe to begin 35 years of God's work in what we now call Germany and Holland, never returning to England. The Pope made him Archbishop of all Germany within the first few years of his arrival. He spent a lot of time travelling around, encouraging members of the new churches he had set up, appointing new leaders and negotiating with local politicians. He is well known for his energy and his perseverance.

When Bible students read of Boniface and the incident with the felling of the sacred tree, they can't help calling to mind the great contest between the Old Testament prophet Elijah and the prophets of Baal on Mount Carmel. Boniface, like Elijah, felt that he needed to counter the superstitious beliefs of the people he met. He felt confident enough of God's power to issue a direct challenge. In Elijah's case, the bull sacrifice was engulfed in flames. In Boniface's case, it was the lack of a lightning bolt from Thor that persuaded the onlookers to listen to him, and led to their conversion to Christianity.

A further part of the account may be legendary but could point to the quick-wittedness of Boniface. Rather like Jesus in his parables, Boniface used a simple illustration to explain a deeper truth. A fir tree that he spotted in the roots at the base of the tree dedicated to Thor inspired him to explain about the embracing love of God from heaven. Because of this, he is credited with the idea of using a fir tree at Christmas to remind us of the coming of Jesus into the world. This can be seen as typical of the way in which pagan traditions were Christianised by giving them a new meaning: the Frisians' belief in a tree dedicated to their god was replaced with a belief in God's love for us, symbolised by a tree. In his explanation,

Boniface allegedly said, 'This humble tree's wood is used to build your homes: let Christ be at the centre of your households. Its leaves remain evergreen in the darkest days: let Christ be your constant light. Its boughs reach out to embrace and its top points to heaven: let Christ be your comfort and your guide.'

There is a shrine dedicated to Boniface at the Roman Catholic Church in Crediton, Devon.

Suggestions for visual aids and resources

- A map of Europe with sticky pads to label the countries Britain, Holland, Germany and Denmark and the British county of Devon
- Two pictures of trees, one of them a fir tree

Ideas for exploring the theme

Ask if the children know the origins of the days of the week. The sun and moon give their names to two of the days, but the others come from the names of gods that were popular in northern Europe before Christianity spread across the region. The gods Woden, Thor and Freya have all given their names to days of the week. In today's assembly you will hear the name Thor, which gives us the word 'Thursday'.

Today's story takes us back to Saxon times. The Saxons came to Britain from Saxony in Germany in the fifth and sixth centuries, but our story is about a man called Boniface, who was born in England about AD670–680.

Show the map and ask the children to assist in naming the countries marked by the labels. The region of the Saxons is now part of Holland and Germany. Point out the county of Devon: perhaps children may have been on holiday here. Boniface was born in Crediton, which is a small town in Devon. His name was Wynfrith: only later was he given the name of Boniface by the Pope.

Refer to the biography of Boniface's life in the 'Key background information', choosing as much of the detail as appropriate. Comment that it is good to hear about a person who made such a difference by not giving up. Boniface didn't get off to a very strong start but he persevered until he succeeded in what he felt God was telling him to do. If he failed at first, he simply thought about it some more, prepared again and then worked hard to succeed. There's a message there for us today!

Suggestions for songs

- Give me oil in my lamp (CP 43)
- The journey of life (CP 45)
- One more step (CP 47, JP 188)
- The Lord's Prayer (CP 5, JP 1921)
- The building song (Ev'rybody's building) (CP 61)
- You've got to move (CP 107)

Suggested prayers

Thank you for the stories from the life of Boniface. Thank you for reminding us of the message that we shouldn't give up. Thank you for giving Boniface the strength to keep going when life was tough, and thank you that you can help us too. Amen

Eternal God, the refuge and help of all your children, we praise you for all you have given us, for all you have done for us, for all that you are to us. In our weakness, you are our strength; in our darkness, you are light; in our sorrow, you are comfort and peace. We cannot number your blessings; we cannot declare your love: for all your blessings we bless you. May we live as in your presence, love the things that you love, and serve you in our daily lives; through Jesus Christ our Lord. Amen

A PRAYER OF ST BONIFACE

— Barnabas —

What's in a name?

Date: 11 June
Theme: Faith in action (Bible disciples)
Curriculum links: PSHE, Geography

We are all aware of how easily the wrong words can hurt others and how our tongues can lead us into all sorts of trouble. This assembly focuses on Barnabas, who was well known as a teacher and encourager. Barnabas is linked strongly with Paul in Paul's first missionary journey. Barnabas was confident that God loved him and he was happy to do God's work. Both Barnabas and Paul changed their names: Paul from Saul and Barnabas from Joseph. How special it must have been to be given a name that meant 'encourager', in terms of building up people in their faith and choosing the right words to make people feel positive about themselves.

Bible story

Joseph was one of the followers who had sold a piece of property and brought the money to the apostles. He was a Levite from Cyprus, and the apostles called him Barnabas, which means 'one who encourages others'.

ACTS 4:36–37

Bible links

Barnabas went to Tarsus to look for Saul. He found Saul and brought him to Antioch, where they met with the church for a whole year and taught many of its people. There in Antioch the Lord's followers were first called Christians.

ACTS 11:25–26

Paul and Barnabas spoke in the Jewish meeting place in Iconium, just as they had done at Antioch, and many Jews and Gentiles put their faith in the Lord.

ACTS 14:1

God has also given each of us different gifts to use. If we can prophesy, we should do it according to the amount of faith we have. If we can serve others, we should serve. If we can teach, we should teach. If we can encourage others, we should encourage them. If we can give, we should be generous. If we are leaders, we should do our best. If we are good to others, we should do it cheerfully.

ROMANS 12:6–8

You must encourage and help each other, just as you are already doing.

1 THESSALONIANS 5:11

Key background information for the teacher

The apostles of the early Church were involved in spreading the good news about Jesus. Some worked among the Jewish people and some worked among those who were not of the Jewish faith. Jewish leaders banned their people from mixing with those outside the Jewish faith, and some of the most important Christian leaders in Jerusalem weren't certain about whether or not they should take the gospel to non-Jewish people. They sent Barnabas to find out what was going on. Barnabas was convinced that everyone should hear about Jesus, as long as it was being done properly and the message was correct.

The most famous person spreading the news to those outside the Jewish faith was Paul, who himself was a Jew—so Barnabas knew that he needed to find Paul and ask his advice. When Barnabas met Paul, he was convinced that what Paul was doing was all part of God's big plan to let the world know about Jesus. Paul agreed to work with Barnabas and, as a team, they travelled about, teaching people about Jesus.

Barnabas recognised that Paul was cleverer than he was, and better at persuading people to become Christians, but there's no sign that he was ever jealous of the attention Paul got. They only argued once, and worked separately for a while, but had a strong record of working together in Antioch. Most of the time, Barnabas just encouraged Paul to get on with the job God had given him to do. In this way, Barnabas fulfilled the nickname he had been given when his name was changed from Joseph to Barnabas, 'the encourager'.

There is an established Roman Catholic tradition of giving an extra name at confirmation. If you have children from Roman Catholic families in school, this would be a useful link to explore.

Suggestions for visual aids and resources

• A baby name book

Ideas for exploring the theme

Ask the children if they know what their names mean. Choose some examples from the baby name book or use the examples below to explain that many names have meanings. Some names come from the Bible or are the names of saints. Many parents name their baby after a grandparent or simply choose a name because it sounds good alongside the surname. In some families, one particular name is used frequently as a middle name. Many parents use a baby name book to search for names they like, and most books explain where the name comes from or what it originally meant. For example:

- Sophie means 'wise'
- Helen means 'light'
- William means 'strong defender'
- Joshua means 'God saves' and is the name of a judge and leader of God's people in the Old Testament

Continue by talking about nicknames. Sometimes nicknames are linked to the jobs that people do, such as Chip for a carpenter or Sparky for an electrician. Sometimes they are linked to qualities that people show or something that has happened to them. Jesus gave his disciples James and John the nickname 'Sons of Thunder', and Simon was nicknamed Peter, meaning 'the rock'. The man in our story today was given a nickname. Originally, his name was Joseph but he was so good at seeing the best in people and saying words that encouraged them that he was called Barnabas, which meant 'son of encouragement'. What a great nickname!

Continue by sharing as much of the background information as is appropriate for the age of the children.

We all know that words can make us feel happy or sad. Smile if you hear something that would make you feel good, and frown if what you hear makes you feel sad.

- 'Your hair looks good today.'
- 'You played well in the match today.'
- 'Your team's rubbish.'
- 'Well done, a super answer.'
- 'If you play with her, I won't be your friend.'
- 'You're really good at that!

Wouldn't it be great if we tried to make sure we said ten positive things to people each day and saw what a difference it makes? It would be a great way to live if, every time we thought of something positive, we said it; and if, when we knew we were about to say something unkind, we stopped ourselves. Paul recognised what an important gift Barnabas had, and encouraged the churches he set up to make a real effort to develop that gift themselves. In his letter to the Roman Christians, he listed encouragement alongside gifts like serving and teaching, because he valued people who made this their habit and allowed God to let this pattern grow in their lives.

Suggestions for songs

• The building song (Ev'rybody's building) (CP 61)

Suggested prayer

Pause and invite the children to think what they appreciate about a particular friend, then finish with the following prayer.

Thank you for the kindness our friends show to us. Thank you for those people who have the gift of encouraging other people to do their best. Help us to let this pattern of friendship grow in our lives, just like Barnabas did. Amen

⊕

Our Father in heaven

Date: Usually second or third Sunday in June
Theme: Special days and celebrations
Curriculum link: PSHE

This assembly focuses on God as the Father of Jesus. Jesus invited everyone who followed his teaching to join his family. Jesus' friends and family are expected to follow in the family likeness in the way they behave towards others and towards God as Father.

Bible story

Jesus' mother and brothers came and stood outside. Then they sent someone with a message for him to come out to them. The crowd that was sitting around Jesus told him, 'Your mother and your brothers and sisters are outside and want to see you.' Jesus asked, 'Who is my mother and who are my brothers?' Then he looked at the people sitting around him and said, 'Here are my mother and my brothers.'

MARK 3:31–34

Bible links

Jesus told her, '… Tell my disciples that I am going to the one who is my Father and my God, as well as your Father and your God.'

JOHN 20:17

God's Spirit doesn't make us slaves who are afraid of him. Instead, we become his children and call him our Father.

ROMANS 8:15

Key background information for the teacher

For many people, the celebration of Fathers' Day is an opportunity to recognise the role that fathers play in our lives. Some children may not live with or be in touch with their fathers. For Christians, Fathers' Day is an opportunity not only to celebrate the best aspects of parenting and to set right any aspects of our relationship with our earthly parents, but also to recognise the key role of God as Father and, in particular, the Father of Jesus.

Suggestions for visual aids and resources

- Photos from the Internet of celebrity parents and children
- The teacher's own picture of their parent or child
- A copy of the love letter from God the Father to his family, from www.fathersloveletter.com (optional)

Ideas for exploring the theme

Ask the children to put up a hand in response to questions about their families—for example, do they have a sister or a brother, do they live with their mum and dad, or just their mum, or just their dad, and so on until everyone has responded to at least one question. Make the point that we are all part of families, which come in all sorts of patterns.

Explain how people sometimes say we look like or remind them of another member of our family. They might say, 'She looks just like her mum!' or 'He's got his grandad's ears!' They might even complain that we've learnt all our worst habits from our parents, or maybe we smile like our mum, fiddle with our ears like our dad, or like the same music as our uncle.

Show the photo of yourself and a relative, or pictures of famous celebrities and their children taken from a magazine or the Internet. Comment on family resemblances or perhaps the way children sometimes follow in the family profession or hobby.

In the Bible, Jesus talked about his dad a lot, saying that people who met him would have a clear idea of what God was like, and that he said and did whatever God his Father told him.

Introduce the Bible story for today. Explain that Jesus was busy teaching and, when his mother and brothers and sisters arrived, the house was packed with people who were listening to Jesus. They had to pass a message to Jesus to let him know his family were outside. Jesus must have realised that he had lots of important things to say and do: he couldn't really go back and live with his mother. His comment to the crowd told them that his family wasn't just his mother and brothers and sisters, but every person who tries to live God's way.

Jesus had a human family—his relatives—but he also had his family of friends and followers who believed that he was the Son of God. The Bible tells us that everyone who follows Jesus' teaching can call themselves a part of God's family. In fact, Jesus went even further by saying that we can call God 'Abba', which is the Aramaic word for 'Daddy'.

If appropriate, read part of the letter from www.fathersloveletter. com as a meditation.

Just as Jesus was like his heavenly Father, so Christians try to behave towards others in a way that shows they are part of the God's family—the biggest and most amazing family on earth.

Suggestions for songs

- Our Father, who art in heaven (CP 51)
- Love divine (HON 321)
- A new commandment (HON 4)
- Make me a channel (OSS 81, JP 161)
- Praise, my soul, the king of heaven (HON 433)
- Father God, I wonder (HON 119)
- Father, we place into your hands (HON 97)

Suggested prayer

Father God, thank you for sending Jesus to show us more clearly what you are like. Help us to remember what he taught and to follow his example of care for others, as well as his example of respecting you, his Father. Help us to do our best to live your way. Thank you that we too can be part of your family. Amen

The Lord's Prayer would also be suitable.

⊕

Saying thank you

Date: 16 June
Alternative date: 3 April
Theme: Saints of Britain
Curriculum links: History, Geography

Richard of Chichester gives us a great example of commitment and perseverance, living out the gospel message. When he was appointed bishop, but was not allowed by the king to move into his palace, he decided to get on with the job anyway and travelled around doing God's work. Although he was a bishop for only eight years, he gained a strong reputation for his care of people. He made sure people didn't go without food and prayed for several hours each day. He prayed hard and worked hard. He put his energies into what he thought would please Jesus and lived out the belief that perseverance is a precondition for a living a fruitful life.

Bible story

'Stay joined to me, and I will stay joined to you. Just as a branch cannot produce fruit unless it stays joined to the vine, you cannot produce fruit unless you stay joined to me. I am the vine, and you are the branches. If you stay joined to me, and I stay joined to you, then you will produce lots of fruit. But you cannot do anything without me... Stay joined to me and let my teachings become part of you. Then you can pray for whatever you want, and your prayer will be answered. When you become fruitful disciples of mine, my Father will be honoured.'

JOHN 15:4–5, 7–8

Bible links

Jesus told the people who had faith in him, 'If you keep on obeying what I have said, you truly are my disciples.'
JOHN 8:31

Don't get tired of helping others. You will be rewarded when the time is right, if you don't give up.
GALATIANS 6:9

God is the one who began this good work in you, and I am certain that he won't stop before it is complete on the day that Christ Jesus returns.
PHILIPPIANS 1:6

You know that many runners enter a race, and only one of them wins the prize. So run to win!
1 CORINTHIANS 9:24

Do everything without grumbling or arguing. Then you will be the pure and innocent children of God. You live among people who are crooked and evil, but you must not do anything that they can say is wrong. Try to shine as lights among the people of this world, as you hold firmly to the message that gives life. Then on the day when Christ returns, I can take pride in you. I can also know that my work and efforts were not useless.
PHILIPPIANS 2:14–16

I know what it is to be poor or to have plenty, and I have lived under all kinds of conditions. I know what it means to be full or to be hungry, to have too much or too little. Christ gives me the strength to face anything.
PHILIPPIANS 4:12–13

Do as God does. After all, you are his dear children. Let love be your guide. Christ loved us and offered his life for us as a sacrifice that pleases God.

EPHESIANS 5:1–2

Key background information for the teacher

Richard of Chichester is probably best remembered for his famous prayer, which focuses on Jesus as his redeemer, friend and brother. Though he was far from perfect, Richard has a lot to say to us today in his example of living a simple life of prayer and generosity. We would find it difficult to condone his involvement in promoting the final Crusade to regain Jerusalem, but in this he was very much a man of his time and was probably following orders that came from the leaders of the Church in Rome. We would not approve of all his actions but we can recognise that, despite his weaknesses, he showed Jesus' love to those he met.

After Richard died in April 1253, many pilgrims came to visit his shrine in Chichester Cathedral and miracles were recorded as people prayed there. Only nine years later, in 1262, the Church authorities in Rome declared that he should be named a saint.

The Diocese of Chichester website is very useful as a reference point (www.diochi.org.uk).

Suggestions for visual aids and resources

• Pictures of road signs from the Highway Code or the Internet, including roadworks, falling rocks, diversion, a gradient, slippery road, and no entry

Ideas for exploring the theme

Show the road signs to the children and ask what they mean. Talk about the shapes: circles are used for orders, triangles for warnings, and rectangles for information. Point out that roads can be full of hazards and it is important that we are ready to react in the right way when things go wrong and we are faced with problems. It is the same in the rest of life. How we tackle the difficulties we meet depends on the training we get at home and school. For Christians, the way they react will reflect the way they try to live their lives to please God.

Explain that the story today is about a man called Richard, who kept on doing God's work when opposition came. Richard lived about 750 years ago. He loved studying and went to Oxford University; yet, when his brother needed his help to run the family farm, he went back to help and continued his studies later. Richard was lucky enough to be taught by a very clever man called Edmund of Abingdon and, after travelling all over Europe to study, he was invited back to become Chancellor of the university—the top job.

When Edmund became Archbishop of Canterbury, he chose Richard to become the next bishop of Chichester. The Pope, who was head of the Church, agreed, but King Henry III had wanted someone else to be bishop, so he refused to let Richard live in the bishop's palace at Chichester. Instead of grumbling and wasting a lot of energy arguing with the king, Richard spent two years living with different people in the area and getting on with the job. He quickly built up a reputation for looking after people, although he could be quite strict if he thought that people, especially the vicars, weren't doing their jobs properly. He is described as someone who tried hard to follow Jesus' teaching and example and was not put off by what other people thought or did.

After two years, the king gave in and allowed Richard to live in Chichester, where he carried on serving God and the people. In fact, he worried some of the other church leaders there by spending a lot of money on helping poor people and giving food to hungry people who came to the cathedral.

Refer back to the road signs. Richard of Chichester was someone who faced lots of obstacles in his life as a bishop. He spent hours praying and studying, then went out to serve people in a way that he thought would make Jesus pleased with him. He used the Bible as his 'highway code' and refused to be put off doing what he believed was right. He must have got fed up at times but, instead of grumbling, he found ways round the obstacles and put his energies into doing God's work.

It is said that, as he was dying, Richard asked to see an image of Jesus on the cross, and he said a prayer of thanks to Jesus for dying for him. We are not sure exactly when in his life he said or wrote the prayer for which he is remembered, but it is a prayer that reminds Christians of Jesus as a friend and Saviour. In the prayer, Richard asks to know God more, to love God more and to follow his ways ever more closely.

Tell the children that you are going to close the assembly with Richard of Chichester's prayer for them to listen to and think about.

Suggestions for songs

- Our Father, who art in heaven (CP 51)
- Love divine (HON 321)
- A new commandment (HON 4)
- Make me a channel (OSS 81, JP 161)

Suggested prayer

Thanks be to thee, my Lord Jesus Christ,
For all the benefits which thou has given me,
For all the pains and insults which thou has borne for me.
O most merciful Redeemer, Friend, and Brother,
May I know thee more clearly,
Love thee more dearly,
Follow thee more nearly.
RICHARD OF CHICHESTER

— Alban —

A soldier and saint

Date: 22 June
Alternative date: 20 March for Roman Catholic Christians
Theme: Saints of Britain
Curriculum link: History

This assembly explores the cost of being a Christian as it looks at the first believer in Britain to be put to death because of his beliefs. It focuses on standing up for what we believe to be right, and children will be able to relate this concept to their own lives, whether in a religious context or not.

Bible story

'God blesses those people who are treated badly for doing right. They belong to the kingdom of heaven. God will bless you when people insult you, ill-treat you, and tell all kinds of evil lies about you because of me.'
MATTHEW 5:10–11

Bible links

He will take the punishment for… others.
ISAIAH 53:11

I honestly expect and hope that I will never do anything to be ashamed of. Whether I live or die, I always want to be as brave as I am now and bring honour to Christ.
PHILIPPIANS 1:20

Key background information for the teacher

Alban was a soldier serving the Roman army in Verulamium, Britain, during the third century AD. Some traditions say that he was born in Britain but this is uncertain. The historian Bede wrote a record of Christians who had died for their faith and dates Alban's death to AD304, though this date is disputed by some modern historians, who place him between 50 and 100 years earlier. Persecution by Rome was a feature of church life in these early years of the established Church.

The story goes that Alban was at home one day when there was a great knocking at the door. A man in a hooded cloak begged to be let in because he was being chased by soldiers who knew that he was a Christian. 'Please hide me!' he cried. In the hours that followed, the man, who was a Christian priest, told Alban all about Jesus and what was so special about him. Alban was fascinated and said that he believed. As a new Christian, he was baptised by the priest.

Word somehow reached the Roman governor of Verulamium that Alban was sheltering a Christian priest, and other soldiers were sent to his home. Alban thought quickly and said to his friend, 'Give me your cloak. Be quick about it! You wear mine and, while I'm talking to them, slip away out of the other door.' Alban pretended to be the priest and was marched away to the governor. The governor recognised him when he removed his hood and was furious that he'd been deceived. The governor offered Alban a deal: 'If you worship the Roman gods, I'll let you go, even though you let the priest escape!'

Alban's reply has become famous: 'I worship and adore the true and living God who created all things.' The Romans tried whipping him to see if he would change his mind but he stuck to his new beliefs.

Alban was given the same punishment as the priest would have received. He was led out of the town and up a small hill, where he was made to kneel down and was beheaded. It is said that a cathedral was built on the exact spot and, once the Romans were gone, the town was renamed St Albans. Alban is often pictured holding a sword to show that he was a soldier, and a palm branch or a cross as a symbol of being martyred for his beliefs. It was not long afterwards that the Roman Emperor Constantine relaxed the rules and it became acceptable to be a Christian in the Roman Empire.

The story lends itself well to role play and could be prepared in advance by a group of children.

Suggestions for visual aids and resources

- A cloak (with a hood if possible)
- Disguises, such as a false moustache or a wig from a party shop
- Pictures of celebrities from magazines, 'off duty' or trying not to be noticed
- A picture of St Alban holding a sword and palm branch

Ideas for exploring the theme

Ask the children if they have ever dressed up as someone else, perhaps for a party or a fancy dress parade. Ask about their disguises and the costumes they wore. You could have some fun with any party shop accessories you have managed to find. Explain that you are going to tell (or watch acted out) a story in which dressing up as someone else wasn't just for fun; it was a matter of life or death.

Now use the story as presented in the 'Key background information' above.

As you conclude, draw out the idea that Alban had made a promise to follow Jesus and would not go back on his promise. In the same way, if we know in our hearts that something is right, we should explain it to people politely and remain faithful to our belief. For instance, we might know it is right to stop someone being bullied on the village sports field or not to join in when people say unkind things about someone in the playground. Alban is an example of someone who was loyal to God and the promise he had made to a friend.

Suggestions for songs

- I'm special (JP 106, TS 222, KS 162)

Suggested prayer

Loving God, help us to be willing to stand firm when we believe that something is right—even when others laugh at us. Help us to be willing to look after people in trouble and help us to be polite to people who are different from us. Please be with the people who are bullied in the world today for what they believe. Amen

— Peter (1) —

Peter's great idea

Date: 29 June
Theme: Faith in action (Bible disciples)
Curriculum link: PSHE

This assembly focuses on someone who had carefully watched Jesus at work and come to the conclusion that he was God's chosen king—the Messiah who would rescue God's people. A fisherman by trade, Peter must have been used to looking for signs in the weather in order to judge the best times and places to fish. He was clearly very observant and often seemed to act as the spokesperson for the other disciples as they travelled together with Jesus.

Bible story

When Jesus and his disciples were near the town of Caesarea Philippi, he asked them, 'What do people say about the Son of Man?' The disciples answered, 'Some people say you are John the Baptist or perhaps Elijah or Jeremiah or some other prophet.' Then Jesus asked them, 'But who do you say I am?' Simon Peter spoke up, 'You are the Messiah, the Son of the living God.' Jesus told him: Simon, son of Jonah, you are blessed! You didn't discover this on your own. It was shown to you by my Father in heaven.

MATTHEW 16:13–17

Bible links

Each of you has been blessed with one of God's many wonderful gifts to be used in the service of others. So use your gift well. If you have the gift of speaking, preach God's message. If you have the gift of helping others, do it with the strength that God supplies. Everything should be done in a way that will bring honour to God because of Jesus Christ, who is glorious and powerful for ever. Amen

1 PETER 4:10–11

Just as shepherds watch over their sheep, you must watch over everyone God has placed in your care... God cares for you, so turn all your worries over to him.

1 PETER 5:2, 7

Always live as God's holy people should, because God is the one who chose you, and he is holy.

1 PETER 1:15

Key background information for the teacher

Today's Bible story is a pivotal point in the Gospel narrative, when people are beginning to notice Jesus and his fame is spreading. People are questioning who he actually is. Is he a teacher, a prophet or a healer—or, indeed, is he the promised Messiah? Peter's response to Jesus' question, 'But who do you say I am?' is sometimes described as Peter's 'great confession', which reflects an older definition of the word 'confession' as a statement of belief.

Suggestions for visual aids and resources

- Items with which to play Kim's game
- Spot-the-difference drawings from a child's puzzle book
- A willing member of staff or an older child

Ideas for exploring the theme

Start the assembly by singing together a song of your choice. Prearrange for a member of staff to enter the hall and talk to you while the children are singing, and then to leave. When the song is over, ask the children if they noticed who entered the hall. Ask further questions: can they describe what the person was wearing, how they had done their hair, whether they were wearing glasses, and so on.

Next, either display a spot-the-difference drawing for the children to examine, or play Kim's game, using two volunteers to inspect the tray before and after you have removed an item. Ask the children how carefully they look at the things and people around them.

When Jesus chose the friends who would help him in his work, they must have wondered what sort of life they would live as they travelled with him. It certainly wasn't dull! They must have watched Jesus carefully, becoming more amazed at the gathering crowds and the wonderful things he said and did. Explain that, as Jesus' fame grew, more people were wondering exactly who he was and where his special power came from.

Comment that Peter was clearly someone who watched carefully and worked out exactly who Jesus was. Perhaps his job as a fisherman, in which he had to check the boat, the nets, the weather and so on, had helped him to practise this skill. It made him even more convinced that he had made the right decision to follow Jesus and learn from him.

What was it that convinced Peter that Jesus was God's Messiah, the person the Jewish people were waiting for? Was it the way Jesus taught with such authority? Was it the size of the crowds or their reaction? Was it the healings he had seen Jesus do? Was it the claims Jesus made about himself, such as having the authority to forgive people's sins?

Peter watched and learned more and more from Jesus and later helped to develop the early Christian Church. He wrote two letters, full of teaching about Jesus. They remind people to keep watch and stay awake, so that they can become good leaders and strong Christians who know all they can about Jesus and show in their lives that they love him. (Read some of the selected verses from the 'Bible links' above, if desired.) Jesus changed Peter from a very observant fisherman into one of the finest leaders of his new Church.

Suggestions for songs

- The building song (Ev'rybody's building) (CP 61)
- I will build my church (TS 259)
- The wise man built his house upon the rock (KS 336)
- Don't build your house on the sandy land (KS 40)
- Cast your burdens on to Jesus (TS 170, KS 107)

Suggested prayer

Thank you that Peter was very good at observing the people around him, especially Jesus. Help us to notice what is going on around us, too, so that we can say the right words and do all we can to help others. Amen

⊕

Rock solid

Date: 29 June
Theme: Faith in action (Bible disciples)
Curriculum link: Design Technology, Science, PSHE

The apostle Peter is a particularly important character for a great variety of reasons. For Roman Catholics, the Pope is considered to stand in direct descent from Peter, whom Jesus commissioned to establish his Church. Much is also made of Peter's simple background and impatience as well as the fact that he denied Jesus after Jesus' arrest. Despite all this, Jesus could see through Peter's human weaknesses and, perhaps because Peter was so aware of his own failings, gave him an important role to play, knowing that he would have to rely on God to get it right.

Bible story

'I will call you Peter, which means "a rock". On this rock I will build my church, and death itself will not have any power over it. I will give you the keys to the kingdom of heaven, and God in heaven will allow whatever you allow on earth. But he will not allow anything that you don't allow.'

MATTHEW 16:18–19

Bible link

When Jesus and his disciples had finished eating, he asked, 'Simon son of John, do you love me more than the others do?' Simon Peter answered, 'Yes, Lord, you know I do!' 'Then feed my lambs,' Jesus said. Jesus asked a second time, 'Simon son of John, do you love me?' Peter answered, 'Yes, Lord, you know I love you!' 'Then take care of my sheep,' Jesus told him. Jesus asked a third time, 'Simon son of John, do you love me?' Peter was hurt because Jesus had asked him three times if he loved him. So he told Jesus, 'Lord, you know everything. You know I love you.' Jesus replied, 'Feed my sheep.'

JOHN 21:15–17

Key background information for the teacher

In the Christian calendar, Peter shares a saint's day with the apostle Paul. These two people did a lot to establish the new Church, both in Jerusalem and around the known world. Peter focused mainly on Jewish followers, some of whom gathered in Jerusalem for festivals and then spread out, back to their own countries. Jesus changed Peter's name from Simon to Peter as a sign that he would be a rock on which to establish the Church (the Greek for 'rock' being *petra*).

Suggestions for visual aids and resources

- Building blocks and playing cards
- Pictures of brick bonds
- Picture of a dry stone wall
- Two tables

Exploring the theme

Place some building blocks on one table and playing cards on the second table. Ask for two volunteers to try to build a tower as high as possible with the blocks and the cards, while you draw out the idea that God uses different people to build and expand his church family. If an exposed brick wall is on show in the hall, you could also look at the brick bonds and how they are put together. Alternatively, show or project pictures of different brick bonds. Ask the children if they have ever seen an extension being built on a house, and explain the importance of getting the foundations solid before building upwards. Some children will be familiar with dry stone walls. Show a picture of a dry stone wall and point out that it takes a skilled builder to place each differently shaped stone where it will fit best.

Explain that Jesus chose a group of people to be his close friends and to help him as he travelled around, teaching people about God and healing those who were unwell. Jesus promised his friends that, while he was with them and when he was no longer with them, God would help them to do the same if they relied on his power. Jesus chose Peter, James and John as his closest friends, and it was to Peter that he gave the task of being like a shepherd to the new Christians, and the first person to begin building the new church. Explain that the word 'church' doesn't mean a building (the first groups of believers met in each other's homes); it means the group of people who believe that Jesus is the Son of God.

Peter was someone who tended to speak first and think later. After Jesus had been arrested, he said that he didn't even know Jesus, yet Jesus could see Peter's potential as a church builder. Refer back to the building blocks and the cards on the tables and expand on the theme that each block or card represents a person in God's Church. Some are reliable building materials, while some are more flimsy. Peter was given the job of starting off this enormous building programme by making sure that Jesus' teaching was shared and that people heard about Jesus' death and resurrection and the coming of the Holy Spirit. Today, there are millions of Christians worldwide. On 29 June the church celebrates the life of this very special man, who did the job Jesus asked him to do.

Suggestions for songs

- The building song (Ev'rybody's building) (CP 61)
- I will build my church (TS 259)
- The wise man built his house upon the rock (KS 336)
- Don't build your house on the sandy land (KS 40)

Suggested prayer

Dear God, thank you for Peter, who listened carefully to what Jesus taught him and then shared it with many people. Thank you for his example of relying on you for help. Thank you that you still use all sorts of people who are willing to listen to you. Amen

⊕

— Thomas —

Seeing is believing

Date: 3 July
Theme: Faith in action (Bible disciples)
Curriculum links: Science, PSHE

This assembly looks at a key incident in the life of one of Jesus' closest friends. Thomas was not present when Jesus first appeared to his disciples and would not believe that Jesus had risen from death. However, when Thomas finally sees the risen Jesus, Jesus comments that those who believe without seeing him will be greatly blessed.

Bible story

Although Thomas the Twin was one of the twelve disciples, he wasn't with the others when Jesus appeared to them. So they told him, 'We have seen the Lord!' But Thomas said, 'First, I must see the nail scars in his hands and touch them with my finger. I must put my hand where the spear went into his side. I won't believe unless I do this!' A week later the disciples were together again. This time, Thomas was with them. Jesus came in while the doors were still locked and stood in the middle of the group. He greeted his disciples and said to Thomas, 'Put your finger here and look at my hands! Put your hand into my side. Stop doubting and have faith!' Thomas replied, 'You are my Lord and my God!' Jesus said, 'Thomas, do you have faith because you have seen me? The people who have faith in me without seeing me are the ones who are really blessed!'

JOHN 20:24–29

Bible link

Jesus worked many other miracles for his disciples, and not all of them are written in this book. But these are written so that you will put your faith in Jesus as the Messiah and the Son of God. If you have faith in him, you will have true life.

JOHN 20:30–31

Key background information for the teacher

Jesus put in several appearances after he came back to life. The first that we need to know about for today is when Jesus appeared to a gathering of his closest friends (John 20:19–23). We are left unsure about why Thomas missed this visit, and why he had to wait a whole week for Jesus to reappear in the same way. On this second occasion, Jesus must have known how Thomas had been feeling because he turned straight to Thomas and spoke to him. Some Bible commentators interpret this as showing how Jesus knows about individual needs, temperaments, doubts and misunderstandings: he meets us as we are.

We might wonder whether it was just that Thomas didn't believe his friends had seen Jesus, or that he really didn't believe Jesus could rise to new life. Perhaps he was still too upset about Jesus' death to believe in the resurrection; perhaps he just needed more evidence. Whatever the case, Thomas wanted to touch Jesus for himself before he would believe. Thomas is sometimes portrayed as someone who doubted Jesus, but this should not detract from the fact that he was also quick to declare that Jesus was his Lord and his God when faced with the truth.

Wouldn't it be easier to believe if we could see God? What an advantage Jesus' first disciples had: they were able to see, listen and touch. Those who have not seen Jesus in person are asked to have faith based on the biblical evidence and their experience of God. For Christians, it is more a case of insight than sight.

Suggestions for visual aids and resources

- A beanbag
- A table and four chairs (optional)
- A candle
- Safety matches or a candle lighter

Ideas for exploring the theme

Throw a beanbag to a volunteer and ask him or her to throw it back. Continue throwing for a while and then allow yourself to drop a catch. Ask if you can have another chance. The volunteer will say 'yes' (you hope) and you can comment that you feel better now. Ask the children if they've ever felt left out—for example, if they are unable to go to a party because of illness or family commitments. Explain that today's assembly is about someone who felt left out but got another chance. His name was Thomas and he was one of Jesus' closest friends. Tell the story of Thomas, based on the Bible passage and background information above.

If time allows, set out a table and four chairs. Place a candle on the table. Invite three volunteers to sit at the table, imagining that they are friends of Jesus (leaving one seat empty). Describe how, even though the doors were locked, Jesus arrived and greeted the disciples. Light the candle as a sign of Jesus' presence. Point out the empty chair and explain that Thomas wasn't with the disciples on that night. Later, the others told him that they had seen Jesus, but Thomas wanted to see Jesus himself. Blow out the candle.

Ask the children how they might have felt if they had been Thomas. Pause and then say that perhaps he felt left out. Everyone else had had a special meeting with Jesus. Invite a fourth volunteer to fill the missing place at the table. Explain that, a week later, Jesus appeared again. Relight the candle. Say that after Jesus had greeted the disciples, he turned straight to Thomas and invited him to touch him to check he was really there. Thomas didn't need to.

He simply announced, 'You are my Lord and my God!' Now he knew it was true. Jesus had come back to life.

Today, people don't have the chance to learn about Jesus by seeing him in person. We learn about the world around us because our senses—sight, touch, hearing, smell and taste—give information to our brains. Christians have to make up their minds about who Jesus is without seeing him, but they can read about him in the Bible, listen to what others have to say, and experience him in many ways in church and in the world.

Suggestions for songs

- God knows me (CP 15)
- Come and praise the Lord our King (CP 21)
- Lord of the dance (CP 22)
- Go, tell it on the mountain (CP 24)
- When Jesus walked in Galilee (CP 25)

Suggested prayer

Thank you, Jesus, for all those who have chosen to follow you, even though they cannot see you. Thank you that you offer your friendship and love to all who believe in you. Amen

— Sea Sunday —

Who is this man?

Date: Usually the second Sunday in July
Theme: Special days and celebrations
Curriculum links: Geography, RE

This assembly focuses on the story of the calming of the storm, which is perhaps one of the best-known examples of Jesus showing his power over the natural world. This assembly would also fit into a group of assemblies about the life of Jesus.

Bible story

That evening, Jesus said to his disciples, 'Let's cross to the east side.' So they left the crowd, and his disciples started across the lake with him in the **boat**. Some other **boats** followed along. Suddenly a storm struck the lake. **Waves** started splashing into the **boat**, and it was about to sink. Jesus was in the back of the **boat** with his head on a pillow, and he was **asleep**. His disciples woke him and said, 'Teacher, don't you care that we're about to drown?' Jesus got up and ordered the **wind** and the **waves** to be quiet. The **wind** stopped, and everything was calm. Jesus asked his disciples, 'Why were you afraid? Don't you have any faith?' Now they were more afraid than ever and said to each other, 'Who is this? Even the **wind** and the **waves** obey him!'

MARK 4:35–41

Bible link

Be humble in the presence of God's mighty power, and he will honour you when the time comes. God cares for you, so turn all your worries over to him.

1 PETER 5:6–7

Key background information for the teacher

Many miracles are recorded as part of the story of Jesus. Some of them took place in response to need, such as the time when he turned water into wine at a wedding (John 2:1–11) or when he provided food for 5000 people on a hillside (John 6:1–13). Others showed him restoring people to health, and yet more showed his power over nature. For Christians, all of Jesus' miracles point to his divine nature. In the story of the calming of the storm, seasoned fishermen were frightened by the ferocity of the storm that blew up. They turned to Jesus for help and weren't disappointed. He had to be woken up to still the storm and he chastised the disciples for not having enough faith to believe that, with him, they would be safe.

Suggestions for visual aids and resources

- The Bible story above, or a retelling in a children's Bible such as *The Barnabas Schools' Bible* (Barnabas, 2007)
- Information and ideas on celebrating Sea Sunday can be found on the Mission to Seafarers website: www.missiontoseafarers.org

Ideas for exploring the theme

Explain that you want some help today to tell a story about the disciples of Jesus. You want the children to join in with some actions when they hear particular words in the story.

Practise these responses:

- **Boat** or **boats:** hoisting a sail
- **Wind:** blowing noise
- **Wave** or **waves:** horizontal rippling of hand
- **Asleep:** snoring or hands together resting on cheek, with head tilted

Tell the story using the Bible passage on page 165, pausing at the key words (shown in bold type) to allow for a response. Congratulate the children and thank them for helping you tell the story. Comment that Jesus was an amazing man who had great power, which he used to help people. You could give examples of other types of miracles, such as those mentioned in the 'Key background information' above. Reiterate that Jesus used his God-given power to help people and to guide them towards faith in God. For Christians, Jesus is like a giant signpost pointing to what God is like. By healing, teaching and helping people, Jesus reminds us of the greatness of God's love and care.

Suggestions for songs

- Lord of the dance (CP 22)
- Cast your burdens on to Jesus (TS 170, KS 107)

Suggested prayer

Dear Jesus, thank you that you showed your power in lots of different ways to help the people you met. Please keep safe all the people who work at sea, such as fishermen and sailors on tankers, especially when the weather is dangerous. Amen

⊕

— Swithun —

It never rains but it pours

Date: 15 July
Theme: Saints of Britain
Curriculum links: History, Geography, Science

Superstition doesn't play a part in the lives of Christians. Instead, for Christians, coincidences are likely to be seen not as a matter of luck or fate but, in faith, as the actions of God. However, superstitions are commonly acknowledged in the world around us. The most famous incident in the life of Swithun (also known as Swithin or Svithin) happened after his death and involves an interpretation of events.

Bible story

Sun and moon, and all you bright stars, come and offer praise. Highest heavens, and the water above the highest heavens, come and offer praise. Let all things praise the name of the Lord, because they were created at his command. He made them to last for ever, and nothing can change what he has done. All creatures on earth, you obey his commands, so come, praise the Lord! Sea monsters and the deep sea, fire and hail, snow and frost, and every stormy wind, come, praise the Lord!

PSALM 148:3–8

Bible links

Everyone who honours your name can trust you, because you are faithful to all who depend on you.

PSALM 9:10

You keep me safe, and I always trust you.
PSALM 25:5

You are wonderful, and while everyone watches, you store up
blessings for all who honour and trust you.
PSALM 31:19

Let the Lord lead you and trust him to help.
PSALM 37:5

Key background information for the teacher

St Swithun was born around AD800 and became the bishop of
Winchester after serving as the prior of the monastery there. He
was bishop for ten years, from 852 to 862. He had studied well
and was regarded as one of the most learned men of his time,
teaching both King Aethulwulf of Wessex and his son, Alfred. He
made it a particular project to organise the building and repair of
churches, which in those days were not only places of worship but
also the main places where the community could meet for a variety
of reasons. Swithun also organised the building of a bridge to the
east of the city and supervised it to make sure the work progressed
quickly. It doesn't sound as if he was one to let tea breaks overrun!

Swithun asked to be buried in a simple grave, close to the
cathedral, where the rain from the eaves could drip on him. It
seems, though, that he didn't get his wish for long, because
his body was soon moved inside the cathedral to a much more
elaborate shrine. Legend has it that it started raining on the day
his body was moved, and rained for another 40 days. People have
interpreted this as a sign that Swithun was upset about not getting
the simple, humble burial that he wanted. A superstition then grew
up that whatever the weather was like on 15 July (the day when his
body was 'translated' or moved indoors), the same type of weather
would last for 40 days to come. It is hard to believe that this was

based on any scientific ideas, but perhaps they were having a run of wet summers!

Of course, we have a greater level of knowledge and have our own concerns about the climate, with worries about global warming and the preservation of the ozone layer. Bible scholars would also remind us that the number 40 in the Bible represents a long time rather than a specific number.

Swithun's shrine was destroyed during the Reformation and about 60 churches in the UK are named after him. Although he died on 2 July, his festival is celebrated on the 15th because of the legend associated with this date, when his body was moved.

The rhyme that has been passed down through the centuries about St Swithun is as follows.

St Swithun's day, if thou dost rain,
For forty days it will remain;
St Swithun's day, if thou be fair,
For forty days 'twill rain na mair.

The calendars of France and Belgium, as well as other parts of Europe, include the festivals of 'weather saints' in June and July. For example, a saying from France linked to Saint Gervais is as follows:

Quand il pleut à la Saint Gervais [19 July]
Il pleut quarante jours après.

(When it rains on the feast of Saint Gervais,
It rains and rains for 40 more days.)

Suggestions for visual aids and resources

- An umbrella
- A weather map from a newspaper or the Internet
- Weather sayings, especially the one about St Swithun

Ideas for exploring the theme

Whenever British people get together, it's said that before long they start talking about the weather. Show your umbrella and refer to the weather forecast you saw recently on TV. Introduce some sayings to do with the weather, and rain in particular, such as:

Rain, rain, go away; come again another day.

The rain in Spain stays mainly in the plain.
(FROM THE MUSICAL *MY FAIR LADY*)

Ask for some volunteers to perform the rhyme 'Incy wincy spider'. Explain that today you are going to tell the story of a saint called Swithun, who is often associated with the weather. It is said that whatever the weather is like on 15 July, his special day, it will be the same for 40 days to follow. Retell the story of Swithun from the 'Key background information' above.

Comment that it is hard to believe that this prediction is based on scientific evidence but, at the time when Swithun lived, less was known about science than we know today. All sorts of sayings and superstitions grew up about all sorts of things. Some of them were based on sensible advice, such as 'It's bad luck to walk under a ladder', whereas others are harder to understand—for example, 'You'll get seven years' bad luck if you break a mirror' or 'You shouldn't open an umbrella indoors'.

However interesting and unusual such ideas are, they need not worry us too much. What would Christian believers say about such advice? Think about whether it encourages your safety, for a start. Then think about whether or not it fits in with beliefs about God and his ways. Christians don't believe in superstitions but want God to direct their lives. Having a faith in God means trusting him for what will happen, as well as taking sensible steps to make sure we don't break rules which have been put in place for our safety.

Suggestions for songs

- All things bright and beautiful (CP 3, HON 21)
- We plough the fields (HON 534)
- There is a song for every season (*Songs for Every Season* CD pack, Out of the Ark Music)

Suggested prayer

Dear God, thank you that you provide the different seasons in all their variety for us to enjoy. Thank you for the farmers, working hard at this time of year to grow the food we need. Thank you, too, that we don't need to be superstitious but can trust you because you love us and want the best for each one of us. Amen

Leavers' service

An end-of-year leavers' service is a time to celebrate and acknowledge the contribution of the children, even if some of them have tried your patience! Some gentle remarks hinting that not everyone has yet achieved sainthood can restore an element of balance, but overall the tone needs to be upbeat.

There are certain songs that seem appropriate but it would also be useful to talk to the group of leavers in advance about particular songs they have enjoyed and, if appropriate, choose from these, or vote for the most popular. Also think about well-known songs to help visitors feel included. As part of the service, some children could be chosen to say one or two sentences about their time at the school, such as their first day, topics enjoyed, residential or day visits, friendships, performances, sports events, clubs, anecdotes about teachers, thoughts about moving on, and so on. (These may need to be carefully edited to avoid any potential embarrassment to members of staff or other pupils.)

It is worth considering a gift for the children. Many schools give a foreign language dictionary by arrangement with the secondary school, a geometry set, or a book such as *It's Your Move* (Scripture Union).

Bible story

Jesus called together his twelve apostles and gave them complete power over all demons and diseases. Then he sent them to tell about God's kingdom and to heal the sick. He told them, 'Don't take anything with you! Don't take a walking stick or a travelling bag or food or money or even a change of clothes. When you are welcomed into a home, stay there until you leave that town. If people won't welcome you, leave the town and shake the dust from your feet as a warning to them.' The apostles left and went from village to village, telling the good news and healing people everywhere.

LUKE 9:1–6

Bible links

I pray that the Lord will bless and protect you, and that he will show you mercy and kindness. May the Lord be good to you and give you peace.

NUMBERS 6:24–26

Suggestions for visual aids and resources

• An illustration of the Roman god, Janus

Ideas for exploring the theme

Start with a welcome given by the head teacher or a Year 6 pupil. Follow the welcome with a song from the selection below and then invite Year 6 pupils, as previously arranged, to come up and give their memories of their primary school experience.

Memories from the children can be followed by a brief talk given by the head teacher, a guest speaker, such as the chair of governors, or the Year 6 teacher. A possible theme might be 'Looking back; looking forward'. Using the illustration of the Roman god, Janus, whose head had two faces, one facing forwards and the other backwards, the talk could be based around these two outlooks, ending with an expression of the hope that Year 6 pupils will make the most of all that is ahead without forgetting their time at primary school.

Humour and popular school jokes can be interjected into the talk as appropriate. Poetry could also be used (see suggestions below).

Retell the story about how Jesus sent out his disciples after preparing them for the next step (Luke 9:1–6). They took no possessions with them, but he gave them advice and they relied on what they already knew about him and his message. Children moving on to secondary school have been prepared by their time at primary school in terms of their knowledge, skills and, perhaps most importantly, their attitudes. Tease out how they have been encouraged to be caring of the world and of each other, respectful to adults and thirsty for knowledge and skills; to work hard and to make the most of the opportunities that are presented to them.

The talk may be followed by the presentation of gifts for Year 6 pupils, followed by a final song, such as 'One more step'.

At the end of the service, Year 6 pupils may be permitted to leave with their teacher first while music is being played. Year 6 could then provide a guard of honour at the door as people leave to shake hands or invite guests to stay for refreshments, which could be served by older children.

Suggestions for songs

- One more step (CP 47, JP 188)
- Brother, sister, let me serve you (HON 73)
- I, the Lord of sea and sky (HON 235)
- Thank you, Lord (CP 32) (This song can be adapted for the occasion: 'for all our friends', 'for [name] school', 'for holidays' and so on)
- This is our school (see page 213)
- Leavers' song (*Songs for Every Occasion* CD pack, Out of the Ark Music)
- This day (*Songs for Every Occasion* CD pack)
- Well done! (*Songs for Every Occasion* CD pack)
- He'll be there (*Songs for Every Assembly* CD Pack, Out of the Ark Music)
- Together (*Songs for Every Assembly* CD Pack)

- Living and learning (*Songs for Every Assembly* CD Pack)
- The school rule song (*Songs for Every Assembly* CD Pack)
- Thank you, Lord ('for this day/our school/my life') (*Songs for Every Singing School* CD pack, Out of the Ark Music)

Suggestions for poetry

- 'What teachers wear in bed!' by Brian Moses
- 'The rules that rule the school' by John Foster
- 'Creative writing' by Gervase Phinn
- 'I think my teacher is a cowboy' by John Coldwell
- 'The painting lesson' by Trevor Harvey

(All the above come from *Read Me 1: a poem for every day of the year*, ed. Gaby Morgan, Macmillan)

- 'My teacher' by Steve Turner
- 'The worst school in the world' by Steve Turner

(Both of the above come from *The Day I Fell Down the Toilet* by Steve Turner, Lion Hudson)

- 'Let no one steal your dreams' by Paul Cookson (from *The Works 3: a poet a week*, ed. Paul Cookson, Macmillan)
- 'The last day of school' by Jeff Moss (from *The Works 2: poems on every subject and for every occasion*, eds. Brian Moses and Pie Corbett, Macmillan)

Suggested prayer

This is our school.
Let peace dwell here,
Let the rooms be full of contentment,
Let love abide here,
Love of one another,

Love of mankind,
Love of life itself,
And love of God.
Let us remember that, as many hands build a house,
So many hearts make a school.
Amen
CANADIAN CREED

Lord, thank you for all that Year 6 mean to us as students and friends, and for the privilege we have had in caring for them and for the contribution they have made to the life of our school. Be with them as they move on to a new school. Keep them safe and let their excitement about new opportunities override any worries they might have. Help them to remember that our best wishes go with them and that you are there as a friend when they need you. Amen

Part Two

Ideas for cross-curricular work

The cross-curricular links are listed under specific subject headings but should be regarded as linking across further subject areas and as an opportunity to develop basic Literacy and ICT skills.

⊞

Saints of Britain

Background information for the teacher

What is a saint?

For Christians, the word 'saint' has different levels of meaning. The apostle Paul often referred to the Christians in a particular place as saints, and this is still the way the word is used by many Protestant churches. It can also refer to all the Christians who have died, so all Christians might be considered to be in training to become saints one day. Since the earliest days of the Church, there have been individual Christians whose lives (or deaths) have become renowned and whose stories have been retold. They are heroes within the Christian tradition, people who have come close to God in their own lifetimes and are regarded as exceptional for different reasons.

Most people who are now regarded as saints were not seeking fame but just wanted to live in obedience to God. These saints can be of varying ages, men or women, and from differing walks of life, but each has a story. The most famous are those whose lives tell the most memorable stories. In some cases, the story may have been embroidered over the years—sometimes, such as in the case of St Christopher or St George, so much so that we are no longer certain of the original basis in fact.

In the days when few people could read, the date of a saint's death would often be the day when his or her story would be read to worshippers as an example to follow. Today, we may regard some of these stories as gory, self-centred, arrogant or even racist. Should we, for example, revere those who dropped out of society and spent hours each day in prayer to gain spiritual wisdom? (Some of those who withdrew in this way set up monastic communities which greatly benefited local communities and national leaders.)

In one sense, Christianity is about loving God and our neighbour, and there are many people who have fulfilled this calling down the centuries. In the twelfth century, Bernard of Clairvaux said that a saint should be someone who is 'seen to be good and charitable, using his every gift for the common good... alike to friend and foe. Such a one, being wholly humble, benefits all, is dear to God and man.'

Cross-curricular links

Geography

- Research the history of local churches that have been named after saints, and find out why they gained this link.
- On a map of the British Isles, mark the places linked with well-known saints, including places that the children have studied.

ICT

- Carry out Internet research to discover how the stories of the patron saints of England, Scotland, Wales and Ireland, as well as other saints, are connected to the Christian community in each country.

Literacy

- Write an account in your own words of the people who brought Christianity to Britain and spread the faith here. A second section could explain how others, such as Boniface, trained in Britain and then took the message abroad. This could also link with stories of Christians who use their skills abroad today.

- Write a report about a local church, giving the history of the saint after which it is named.

History

- Organise a visit to a local church and look for clues about saints in the statuary and stained glass. Write a mixture of a recount and a report, explaining the key features of the building.

Art

- Find out about a famous monastic site, especially the practical and spiritual routines undertaken by the monks. Some monks specialised in copying out the Bible. Choose a simple Bible text, such as part of a psalm, and illuminate the first letter in an exaggerated way, surrounding it with objects beginning with that initial letter.
- Many monastic sites specialised in helping people who were unwell, using plants as medicines. Research this topic and draw some of the plants in detail. The herbs will be easy to find. Make a class display with the finished work.

PSHE

- Find out about the work of Christians in Britain and in other countries. How does such work affect the lives of others and the communities in which people live? What motivates people to do this kind of work and what skills are they using?

Drama

- Prepare a weather report and include sayings and superstitions about it. Watch examples on TV and then present the report as a dramatic piece.

RE

- Research the process by which someone is officially given the title of saint.
- Research the life of a modern-day saint and identify how his or her life reflects Jesus' own life and teaching. For suggestions, see Theme 2, 'Faith in Action', and the Bibliography for resources (page 218).

Music

- Find out about music linked to specific areas of the British Isles, especially traditional folk songs and instruments. (See Bibliography for suggested resources.)

⊕

Faith in action

Key background information for the teacher

Many Christians have obeyed Jesus' command to go to people of all nations with the good news of the gospel (Matthew 28:19–20). Some have either been part of religious institutions such as monasteries or have set up organisations such as charities, in order to live out this calling.

Cross-curricular links

ICT

- Research the lives of modern-day Christians, such as Father Cyprian Michael Tansi (a Catholic priest from Nigeria who spread Christian beliefs among his people), Mother Teresa of Calcutta (a Catholic nun, famous for working to relieve suffering among the poor of India), Frances Cabrini (an Italian nun sent to work among poor Italian immigrants in the USA), and Maximilian Kolbe (a Polish priest sent to Auschwitz).

- Research charities that work in the developing world and discuss what equipment would be needed to help refugees or people caught up in a natural disaster such as an earthquake. ('Send a Cow' is an intriguing organisation that does just this.) What is the ongoing need? How do charities aim to meet these needs?

- Contact Christian Aid for their latest pack, or research their work on the Internet. Hold a tea party at school to raise money for Christian Aid, using and promoting Fair Trade products. Produce five fascinating facts about the charity or Fair Trade and place them on the tea tables.

- Research charities that work in Britain. List them, then group them as children's charities, animal charities and those that work to relieve poverty. As a class, choose one to raise money for, and plan events after due discussion with the head teacher.

Drama

- Dramatise the stories of saints such as Christopher, Crispin, George or Alban.

Literacy

- Create written work about the lives of people such as Martin Luther King, Gladys Aylward, Florence Nightingale and George Müller. Should any of these people be given the title of saint? Why or why not?

- Invite a local minister or youth worker to be interviewed. Have an initial discussion, based around the idea of key words to describe the sort of person Jesus was. What sort of things did he do during his lifetime? Prepare questions in advance such as 'What does it mean to be a Christian?' and 'In what ways does a Christian base his or her life on the way Jesus lived?'

History

- Using the material about Martin Luther King on pages 24–27, have a discussion about human rights and racism. Research the work of The United Nations and its statements about human rights and the rights of children.

- Look at the period of the Civil Rights Movement in the USA and discuss how and why people were treated differently.

- So much of what we remember of Martin Luther King is based on one famous speech. Are there others, such as Abraham Lincoln, Winston Churchill or Nelson Mandela, whose speeches are equally famous?

⊕

The life of Jesus

Key background information for the teacher

See also the cross-curricular work for 'Special days and celebrations' (pages 191–199) for ideas about the life of Jesus. Topics associated with the life of Jesus can be completed across one academic year or taken as stand-alone class work (see Bibliography on page 218 for useful resources).

Cross-curricular links

Art

- Research the symbolism of the cross across the world in culture, paintings and sculptures.
- Design a set of posters featuring events in Jesus' life and ministry, or specifically for Holy Week.
- Gather a small selection of pictures of Jesus and discuss how he is presented by different cultures and generations. How do the children picture him?
- Make a collage by sticking coloured fish shapes on to a sheet of A4 card. Write the words 'Jesus said, "Come and eat!"' at the top of the sheet (John 21:12a). Cover the card with coloured netting. Display the work and tell the story of Jesus' breakfast on the beach (John 21:1–14).
- Download the folk story of 'The three trees' from the Internet and illustrate it as a storyboard, or fold your paper to form three sections and design a triptych.

- Take an incident in Jesus' life and present it in the style of a graphic novel.

Drama

- Choose an event in Jesus' life to role play, or give a selection of Bible passages for pupils to present back to the class. In the following example, the number within the brackets suggests how many actors will be needed for each scene, and adds up to a class of about 30.
  - ❖ Luke 5:12–14: Jesus heals a man with leprosy (2)
  - ❖ Luke 5:17–26: Jesus heals a crippled man (6+)
  - ❖ Luke 7:11–17: Jesus raises a widow's son (5+)
  - ❖ Luke 13:10–13: Jesus heals a woman on the sabbath (2)
  - ❖ Luke 17:11–19: Jesus heals ten men with leprosy (11)
  - ❖ Luke 19:1–9: Jesus meets Zacchaeus (4+)

Literacy

- Create an acrostic or mesostic poem based on important words, such as God or Jesus. For example:

miGhty
pOwerful
raDiant

maJestic
rEdeemer
maSter
woUnded
Saviour

- Write a short biography based on Jesus' life. Decide on an audience and make choices about what to include. What is essential to include about Jesus? How much should the author's interests be allowed to influence the content? (It is often suggested that Luke was a doctor and was therefore especially interested in Jesus' healing miracles, for example.) What design should be on the cover?

RE

- Show part or all of a DVD such *The Miracle Maker* to give pupils a full sweep of Jesus' life and ministry.
- The Christian year is structured around Jesus' birth, life, death and resurrection and the fulfilment of the promise of the coming of the Holy Spirit. These key events can be used as an ordering task.

Literacy

- Research the evidence for the resurrection and propose possible suggestions for pupils to investigate, such as 'Jesus never really died', 'The body was stolen', 'Jesus really did rise from the dead', and so on. Is there evidence to support any of these suggestions? How might people argue against any of these statements? Prepare a debate for and against, using Bible passages as well as general statements to back up the arguments.

Drama

- Reenact the court scene in Acts 5:27–32, where the believers had to explain their new faith in front of the leaders of the Jewish people.

Maths

- Research Bible passages that tell of witnesses to the risen Jesus, and add up how many different people saw Jesus. References include 1 Corinthians 15:1–8; Mark 16:9–14; John 20:1–29; John 21:1–2; Luke 24:13–35; Matthew 28:8–9.

Science

- Research how our senses give information to our brains, and relate this to Christian belief about Jesus. Explain that Christians rely on the accounts in the Bible, where the events of Jesus' life and his words are recorded to enable us to learn about Jesus.

⊕

Special days and celebrations

Key background information for the teacher

What we celebrate and why is a very useful question to explore with children. In the past, celebrations were inextricably linked to the religious calendar (the word 'holiday' is based on the words 'holy day'), and there were many more holidays to allow people to attend services at church. The number of religious holidays is now more limited but they still form the core of our holiday system, along with a series of Bank Holidays.

Some holidays were linked to farming, and longer school holidays were taken in parts of the country where the harvest was a major focus.

Some religious celebrations are influenced by the Jewish calendar. For example, the timing of Passover is linked to the phases of the moon, and this continues to dictate the timing of Easter. Similarly, many world religions follow the seasons, and harvest times in particular. Some Christian festivals supplant the dates of pagan festivals. For example, Christmas falls close to the shortest day of the year, when festivals of light and fire were typical, which resonates with Christian belief that Jesus is the light for the world.

The pattern of the Christian year is closely linked to the life of Jesus, so there is an overlap between these two themes.

Cross-curricular links (General)

Literacy

- Introduce the topic by working in groups to list as many celebrations as possible. Discuss which ones are personal and which are linked to milestones in our lives. Can they be divided into religious and non-religious events, or is this a false distinction?
- Write a poem about a birthday party, including ideas for games and food. The ideas could be listed on strips of paper and then shuffled into an order that the group finds pleasing, to create a list poem. This idea could be used as a focus for a particular time of year, such as Christmas or Easter.

RE

- Match descriptions of the celebration with the time in the Christian year. For example:
  - ❖ Advent: Preparation for the coming of Jesus
  - ❖ Christmas: Celebration of Jesus' birth
  - ❖ Epiphany: Revelation of Jesus as the Son of God
  - ❖ Lent: A time of reflection before Easter
  - ❖ Easter: Jesus' death and resurrection
  - ❖ Pentecost: The coming of the Holy Spirit
  - ❖ Trinity: Explanation of the threefold nature of God

Cross-curricular links (Epiphany)

RE

- Who do Christians think Jesus is, and what is the evidence for their belief? What do the titles that people use about him, or that he used about himself, tell us (for example, Lord, Saviour, good shepherd, and so on)?

- What do the wise men's gifts reveal about who they thought Jesus was?

Cross-curricular links (Lent)

PSHE

- Discuss a 'recipe' for a successful life. What would indicate success?

RE

- How do religions such as Christianity measure success?
- Discuss the guidelines that people use to shape their lives and decisions.

Literacy

- Write a recipe poem, using 'ingredients' and the type of imperative verbs found in a recipe. The poem could be about a football match or a pop group, a party or a theatre production. For example, the ingredients needed for a recipe for a football match might be:
  - ❖ pitch of hardwearing grass
  - ❖ referee wearing black and white
  - ❖ four corner posts with flags on top
  - ❖ two teams, one in red, the other in blue
  - ❖ a crowd cheering and chanting
  - ❖ two managers shouting to their players
  - ❖ subs waiting on the bench
  - ❖ Two linesmen running the line
- The imperative verbs might include chop; stir in; fold in; add; roll; mix; pour in; whisk; beat; bake at; serve.

Cross-curricular links (Mothering Sunday)

ICT

- Research examples of mothers in the Bible and write a booklet or prepare a PowerPoint presentation. Possibilities include:
  - ❖ Hagar (Genesis 21:14–16)
  - ❖ The mother of Moses (Exodus 2:1–3)
  - ❖ Hannah (1 Samuel 1:20–28)
  - ❖ The Canaanite woman (Matthew 15:21–28)
  - ❖ Mary (Luke 1:39–56)
  - ❖ Elizabeth (Luke 1:42–45)

Cross-curricular links (Holy Week and Easter)

RE

- Revise the events of Holy Week and put them in order of occurrence. The correct order is:
  - ❖ Sunday: Jesus enters Jerusalem riding on a donkey
  - ❖ Monday–Wednesday: Jesus teaches in the temple
  - ❖ Thursday: Jesus eats the Passover meal with his disciples
  - ❖ Friday: Jesus is condemned to death and nailed to a cross
  - ❖ Sunday: Jesus is raised to life
- Once the children know the events, try to go deeper and explore the feelings of the people involved, perhaps through drama, and discuss the significance of the events on Jesus' overall ministry.
- Write a list of words that link to Easter, and identify common themes. Possibilities might include: donkey, palm, cross, wine, lamb, grave, trial, temple, crowd, bread, Passover, branches, cloaks, Simnel cake, die, crown, pancake, arrest, angel.
- Discuss symbols and how they can speak to us in a variety of ways.

Literacy

- Write a haiku poem with the traditional pattern of three lines set in five, seven and five syllables. A set of haikus on a linked theme is called a renga. You could create a renga, either by one child or by a group. Stick with an Easter theme or span the whole Lent and Easter period. The last line of a haiku is often a comment on the first two lines, so it needs to have impact. For example:

That Sunday morning
Jesus' friends went to his grave
But he had risen!

Easter time is fun.
Celebrate by eating eggs.
Chocolate ones are best!

Let's thank our mums who
Do so much to care for us—
They are fantastic!

- Share poems and songs about Easter and either use them as models for writing or challenge the children to learn one.
- Read texts with the children that link to Easter, such as *The Lion, the Witch and the Wardrobe* by C.S. Lewis (the death of Aslan), *The Selfish Giant* by Oscar Wilde or *The Pilgrim's Progress* by John Bunyan.

Art

- Use the following symbols as a basis for collage or card designs: sword, cockerel, donkey, perfume, silver coins, sponge, dice, spices, nails, Jesus, pebbles, bandage, flower, chick.
- Design a set of pictures or a storyboard based on the events of Holy Week.

- Design a bookmark using a Bible verse associated with Easter, such as John 3:16. Use a template such as a cross shape to fill with the words.
- Show Easter cards to the children so that they can design their own. Other traditional craft ideas might include making Easter bonnets, decorating eggs, or making palm crosses or Easter gardens.

Science

- Discuss the link between the story of Easter and new life in nature. Research animals that lay eggs and those that give birth to live young. Younger children could link a list of animals to their young (for example, goat—kid and so on).

ICT

- Offer a variety of research tasks, such as the use of palms in the Bible, foods eaten at Easter in different countries, how Easter is celebrated round the world, or the ways in which the events of Holy Week and Easter have been dramatised, such as medieval Mystery Plays or the Passion Play at Oberammergau.

Drama

- Dramatise events such as Jesus' arrival at Jerusalem. Encourage the children to annotate the scripts with ideas for positions and gestures. (Some examples are given below to start with, but children may think of their own.)

A: (Moving towards B and C) Have you heard that he's coming?

B: Who is?

A: (Raising eyebrows, looking surprised) Jesus, of course! Fancy not knowing that!

B: I expect he's coming to the Passover Festival like everyone else.

A: Yes, you're probably right. I wonder if he'll speak to the crowds today.

C: *(Leaning in to speak)* I heard him speak a few weeks ago in Galilee.

B: I hear there were hundreds of people there.

C: Yes, there were—but you could have heard a pin drop, people sat so still.

A: He's quite famous now, isn't he? I've heard people say that some of the other rabbis are jealous.

C: Well, he does make learning about God worth listening to. That's more than you can say for some of them.

B: Did he tell people any more about his kingdom?

A: I thought his dad was a carpenter, not a king.

C: If he's a carpenter's son, he's said and done some amazing things!

B: I wonder if he'll heal some more people this week.

C: Here he comes now.

A: Let's try to get nearer the front. I can't see from here.

B: Listen to the crowd… This is going to be quite some Passover.

Crowd shouts are heard: 'Praise God! Jesus! Here comes God's king! Hosanna! Son of David!'

Music

- Make up songs about Easter to be sung to well-known tunes, such as nursery rhymes or folk tunes. An example is 'We have a king who rides a donkey' set to the tune of 'What shall we do with the drunken sailor', to be found in *Someone's Singing, Lord* (A&C Black).

Cross-curricular links (Ascension)

History

- Research customs associated with Ascensiontide. For example, the fifth Sunday after Easter is called Rogation Sunday, and the following Monday to Wednesday are known as Rogation Days. Prayers are often made at this time for the sowing of seed leading to a strong harvest, as well as for farmers with livestock. Find out about the planting of the Penny Hedge on the beach at Boyes Haithe near Whitby, Yorkshire, or the custom of well dressing in Derbyshire. Ascension is also a time when many parishes engage in 'beating the bounds' of the parish, when churchgoers walk around the parish or village boundary.

Drama

- Present the puppet sketch relating to the ascension on pages 117–119.

Cross-curricular links (Pentecost)

History

- Research customs associated with Pentecost, such as the tradition of holding baptisms at this time of year, or cheese rolling at Stilton in Cambridgeshire.

Drama

- Dramatise the story of Pentecost with sound effects and using streamers made from red, yellow and orange crêpe paper.

RE

- Research symbols used in the Bible to denote the Holy Spirit, such as a dove, wind, fire or water, and discuss how Christians find these symbols helpful in understanding the work of God in their lives.
- Read the story of Jesus' baptism (Mark 1:9–11), then discuss the dove as an representation of God's action. Broaden the discussion to think about what Christians believe the Holy Spirit is like.

Art

- Create a banner or altar cloth using a combination of the symbols of the Holy Spirit, or focusing on a single symbol, such as fire.
- Draw a template of a dove and fill it with key words or verses to do with the Holy Spirit. Place a piece of paper on top of the template, secure them together and then write the words and verses around the outline so that you are 'drawing with words'.

Geography

- In many churches, the lectern incorporates a carving of an eagle—a strong bird which is accustomed to covering vast distances with ease. Research how the message of Jesus spread after Peter spoke to the crowds at Pentecost. Use the names of the letters in the New Testament as a guide to places to which the gospel message spread, and record them as labels on a picture of a suitcase.

Design technology

- Bring in kites and then design your own before having a competition to see which one flies the best.
- Make a small clay lamp with a lip at one side and a small hole for a wick.

Science

- Play games that involve creating a breeze. For example, cut out some large fish shapes and curl the tail end slightly. Use rolled up newspapers sealed with tape to flap the air behind the fish shapes, to race them across the floor. This works best on a smooth floor where there is less friction.

Part Three

Appendices

⊕

National Curriculum: Index of related QCA units

This index is correct at the time of going to press. Please also refer to the Non-Statutory National Framework for RE for further related units, and to the DfES Standards website for up-to-date revisions. Of course, each Local Authority develops its own guidance on the teaching of RE, including a suggested syllabus based on its consultation with faith groups, and this should also be accessed. In addition, the approach to the National Curriculum is constantly under review, with a continuing emphasis on basic skills and suggestions for cross-curricular teaching. The ideas for cross-curricular work on pages 180–200 reflect this approach.

Saints of Britain

RE Unit RB: Who were the friends of Jesus?
Geography Unit 24: Passport to the world (Finding out about other places)
History: Unit 6B: Why have people invaded and settled in Britain in the past? (An Anglo-Saxon case study)

Faith in action

RE Unit RB: Who were the friends of Jesus?
RE Unit 1B: What does it mean to belong in Christianity? (Includes baptism)
RE Unit 1F: What can we learn from visiting a church?
RE Unit 2B: Why did Jesus tell stories?

RE Unit 3D: What is the Bible and why is it important to Christians?

RE Unit 3E: What is faith and what difference does it make?

RE Unit 5D: How do the beliefs of Christians influence their actions? (Strong on concepts of neighbour and forgiveness)

RE Unit 6E: What can we learn from Christian religious buildings?

History Unit 20:   What can we learn about recent history from studying the life of a famous person? (This could be based on Martin Luther King, for example)

Citizenship Unit 1:   Taking part (Roles within school life and taking part in decision-making)

Citizenship Unit 2:   Choices (Rights, responsibilities, influences on us and the effect on others of the choices we make)

Citizenship Unit 5:   Living in a diverse world (Includes rights, equality and local communities)

Citizenship Unit 7:   Children's rights: human rights (Respect and responsibility in school and the local community)

Art Unit 2C: Can buildings speak? (Links to church visit)

History Unit 4:   Why do we remember Florence Nightingale?

History Unit 11:   What was it like for children living in Victorian Britain? (Links to the work of George Müller)

The life of Jesus

RE Unit RB: Who were the friends of Jesus?
RE Unit 2B: Why did Jesus tell stories?
RE Unit 3C: What do we know about Jesus?
RE Unit 4C: Why is Easter important for Christians?

Special days and celebrations

RE Unit 1B:	What does it mean to belong in Christianity? (Includes baptism)
RE Unit 3A:	What do signs and symbols mean in religion?
RE Unit 4C:	Why is Easter important for Christians?

⊕

Index of songs and music

Come and Praise: CP
Hymns Old and New: HON
Junior Praise: JP
Kidsource: KS
Our Singing School: OSS
The Rainbow Songbook: RS
The Source: TS

Saints of Britain

A new commandment (HON 4)
All things bright and beautiful (CP 3, HON 21)
Fill thou my life (CP 41)
For all the saints (HON 134)
Give me oil in my lamp (CP 43)
God is working his purpose out (JP 57)
He who would valiant be (CP 44, JP 80)
I'm special (JP 106, TS 222, KS 162)
In Christ there is no east or west (CP 66)
Light up the fire (CP 55)
Love divine (HON 321)
Make me a channel (OSS 81, JP 161)
O Lord, all the world belongs to you (CP 39)
Oh when the saints (OSS 100, JP 195)
One more step (CP 47, JP 188)
Our Father, who art in heaven (CP 51)
Song of Caedmon (CP 13)

Spirit of God (CP 63)
Swing low (OSS 129)
The building song (Ev'rybody's building) (CP 61)
The journey of life (CP 45)
The Lord's Prayer (CP 51, JP 192)
The wise may bring their learning (CP 64)
There is a song for every season (*Songs for Every Season* CD pack,
    Out of the Ark Music)
Travel on (CP 42)
We plough the fields (HON 534)
When I needed a neighbour (CP 65, JP 275)
You've got to move (CP 107)

Faith in action

All glory, laud and honour (HON 11)
All the nations of the earth (CP 14)
As with gladness men of old (HON 41)
At the name of Jesus (CP 58)
Be bold, be strong (TS 38, KS 17)
Cast your burdens on to Jesus (TS 170, KS 107)
Christ the Lord is risen today (HON 80)
Come and praise the Lord our King (CP 21)
Come my brothers, praise the Lord (CP 20)
Cross over the road (CP 70)
Don't build your house on the sandy land (KS 40)
Easter jubilation (*Songs for Every Easter* CD pack,
    Out of the Ark music)
Father, I place (JP 42)
Fill thou my life (CP 41)
For I'm building (JP 47)
From the darkness came light (CP 29)
Gabriel's song (Mary, Mary, you are the one) (see page 212)
Give me oil in my lamp (CP 43)

Go, tell it on the mountain (CP 24)
God knows me (CP 15)
He who would valiant be (CP 44)
He's got the whole world (CP 19)
Hosanna (HON 215)
Hosanna! (*Songs for Every Easter* CD pack, Out of the Ark Music)
I, the Lord of sea and sky (HON 235)
I will build my church (TS 259)
If I had a hammer (OSS 61)
Imagine (OSS 65)
I'm special (JP 106, KS 162, TS 222)
In Christ there is no east or west (CP 66)
Jesus' hands were kind hands (JP 134)
King of kings and Lord of lords (RS 54)
Light up the fire (CP 55)
Lord of the dance (CP 22)
Make me a channel (OSS 81, JP 161)
My God is so big (JP 169)
O Lord, all the world belongs to you (CP 39)
One more step (CP 47, JP 188)
Our Father, who art in heaven (CP 51)
Peace is flowing like a river (HON 412)
Praise him (CP 40)
Reach for the stars (OSS 109)
Shine, Jesus, shine (HON 317)
Spirit of God (CP 63)
Take my life (HON 464)
Tell out, my soul (HON 467)
The angel Gabriel from heaven came (HON 471)
The best gift (CP 59)
The building song (Ev'rybody's building) (CP 61)
The family of man (CP 69)
The journey of life (CP 45)
The Lord's Prayer (CP 51, JP 192)

The wise man built his house upon the rock (KS 336)
The wise may bring their learning (CP 64)
This child (TS 511)
This is the day (HON 508)
Travel on (CP 42)
We have a king who rides a donkey (*Someone's Singing, Lord*, A&C Black)
When a knight won his spurs (CP 50)
When I needed a neighbour (CP 65, JP 275)
When I'm 64 (OSS 164)
When Jesus walked in Galilee (CP 25)
You'll never walk alone (OSS 177)

The life of Jesus

A man for all the people CP 27)
All glory, laud and honour (HON 11)
All the nations of the earth (CP 14)
As with gladness men of old (HON 41)
Christ the Lord is risen today (HON 80)
Come and praise the Lord our king (CP 21)
Crown him with many crowns (HON 103)
Easter jubilation (*Songs for Every Easter* CD pack, Out of the Ark Music)
From the darkness came light (CP 29)
Gabriel's song (Mary, Mary, you are the one) (see page 212)
Go, tell it on the mountain (CP 24)
He is Lord (JP 75)
He's got the whole world (CP 19)
Hosanna (HON 215)
Hosanna! (*Songs for Every Easter* CD pack, Out of the Ark Music)
I'm special (JP 106, KS 162, TS 222)
Jesus, good above all other (CP 23)
Jesus' hands were kind hands (JP 134)

King of kings and Lord of lords (RS 54)
Light up the fire (CP 55)
Lord Jesus Christ (JP 156)
Lord of all hopefulness (JP 157)
Lord of the dance (CP 22)
Praise him (CP 40)
Said Judas to Mary (JP 211)
Seek ye first the kingdom of God (HON 442)
Spirit of God (CP 63)
Take my life (HON 464)
The angel Gabriel from heaven came (HON 471)
The head that once was crowned with thorns (HON 480)
The Lord's Prayer (CP 51, JP 192)
This is the day (JP 255)
This is the day (HON 508)
We have a king who rides a donkey (*Someone's Singing, Lord*, A&C Black)
We three kings (HON 537)
Were you there? (JP 269)
When Jesus walked in Galilee (CP 25)
Who took fish and bread? (JP 286)

Special days and celebrations

A new commandment (HON 4)
Be bold, be strong (TS 38, KS 17)
Bind us together (HON 60)
Brother, sister, let me serve you (HON 73)
Cast your burdens on to Jesus (TS 170, KS 107)
Come and praise the Lord our king (CP 21)
Come, my brothers, praise the Lord (CP 20)
Don't forget (*Songs for Every Easter*, Out of the Ark CD pack)
Father God, I wonder (HON 119)
Father, we adore you (HON 125)

Father, we place into your hands (HON 97)
Fight the good fight (HON 128)
For the beauty of the earth (CP 11)
Forty days and forty nights (HON 145)
Give me oil in my lamp (CP 43)
Give me joy (OSS 44)
God has promised (CP 31)
Go tell it on the mountain (CP 24)
He'll be there (*Songs for Every Assembly* CD Pack,
    Out of the Ark Music)
He's got the whole world (CP 19)
Join with us (CP 30)
I, the Lord of sea and sky (HON 235)
I'm special (JP 106, TS 222, KS 162)
Jesus is Lord (HON 270)
Leavers' song (*Songs for Every Occasion* CD pack,
    Out of the Ark Music)
Let there be love (HON 298)
Living and learning (*Songs for Every Assembly* CD Pack,
    Out of the Ark Music)
Lord of the dance (CP 22)
Love divine (HON 321)
Make me a channel of your peace (OSS 81, JP 161, HON 328)
Now thank we all our God (CP 38, HON 354)
O Lord, all the world belongs to you (CP 39)
O praise ye the Lord (CP 37)
One more step (CP 47, JP 188)
Our Father, who art in heaven (CP 51)
Pancakes (*Songs for Every Season* CD pack, Out of the Ark Music)
Praise him (CP 40)
Praise, my soul, the king of heaven (HON 433)
Praise the Lord in everything (CP 33)
Praise the Lord, you heavens (CP 35)
Thank you, Lord (CP 32)

Thank you, Lord ('for this day/our school/my life…')
　(*Songs for Every Singing School* CD pack, Out of the Ark Music)
The building song (Ev'rybody's building) (CP 61)
The journey of life (CP 45)
The Lord's Prayer (CP 51)
The school rule song (*Songs for Every Assembly* CD Pack,
　Out of the Ark Music)
This day (*Songs for Every Occasion* CD pack, Out of the Ark Music)
This is our school (see page 213)
Together (*Songs for Every Assembly* CD Pack, Out of the Ark Music)
Well done! (*Songs for Every Occasion* CD pack, Out of the Ark Music)
When a knight won his spurs (CP 50)
When Jesus walked in Galilee (CP 25)

Gabriel's song (Mary, Mary, you are the one)

© Martin Cox

(Gabriel)

2. Mary, Mary, gentle and pure,
I know you're not certain, I know you're not sure,
But God's hand is gentle, so please do not fear,
God's Spirit is working—the Lord will be near.

3. Mary, Mary, precious and kind,
God's special woman, put doubting behind;
He can do all things, for great is his love,
So take on his mission, his word from above.

4. As verse 1.

This is our school

© Martin Cox

This is our— school, where we
This is our— school, full of
At x - x — school, we—
This is our— school, it's a

learn to get a - long, — Some-where we know that we — be - long, Learn- ing
books we've learned to — read, — Learn - ing the skills that we — will need, Try - ing
try to show con - cern, — All of us know where we — can turn If we
place be - yond com - pare — Where we en- deavour to show — we care, We will

more a - bout the diff'- rence be-tween what's right and wrong, This is our— school,——
o - ver and — a - gain till we find we will suc - ceed, This is our— school,——
need a help- ing hand, it's a hab - it we have learned, This is our— school,——
trea- sure all — the mem - or - ies of the life we share, This is our— school,——

This is our — school. ——
This is our — school. ——
This is our — school. ——
This is our — school. ——————

This is our — school,

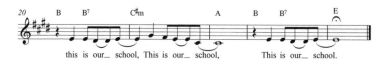

this is our— school, This is our— school, This is our— school.

Reproduced with permission from *Assemblies for Spring and Summer Festivals*, BRF 2010 (978 1 84101 701 3)

www.barnabasinschools.org.uk

Index of Bible passages

All Bible passages quoted are taken from the Contemporary English Version (CEV). If you prefer another version, the references are clearly listed for your convenience. A very useful website where alternative translations can be accessed is www.biblegateway.com.

Bibliography

Music

Come and Praise, ed. Geoffrey Marshall–Taylor (BBC)

Kidsource, ed. Capt Alan Price (Kevin Mayhew)

The Source (Kevin Mayhew)

Carol Praise (Marshall Pickering) (carols linked to the annunciation)

Hymns Old and New (Kevin Mayhew)

The Rainbow Songbook (Word Music UK)

Songs for Every Season, Mark and Helen Johnson (Out of the Ark: CD, Book and Words on Screen packs)

Songs for Every Easter, Mark and Helen Johnson (Out of the Ark: CD, Book and Words on Screen packs)

Songs for Every Occasion, Mark and Helen Johnson (Out of the Ark: CD, Book and Words on Screen packs) (includes a leavers' song)

Songs for Every Singing School, Mark and Helen Johnson (Out of the Ark: CD, Book and Words on Screen packs)

Songs for Every Assembly, Mark and Helen Johnson (Out of the Ark: CD, Book and Words on Screen packs)

Books

Assemblies for Autumn Festivals, Martin Cox (Barnabas, 2007) (See especially further material on Saints of Britain)

Stories of Everyday Saints, Veronica Heley (Barnabas, 2002)

Celtic Blessings, Brendan O'Malley (Canterbury Press, 1998)

Our Poems and No Messin', compiled by Margaret Cooling from a poetry competition (Scripture Union, 1999) (useful sections on Bible people, Easter, God, Jesus and the Holy Spirit as well as several poems on a creation theme, useful in the autumn term)

A Book of Saints, James Cochrane (Aurum Press, 2000)

The Treasury of Saints and Martyrs, Margaret Mulvihill (Marshall, 1999)

Days of the Lord Volume 1 (Advent, Christmas, Epiphany), various authors

A-cross the World, Martyn Payne and Betty Pedley (Barnabas, 2004)

Messiah, Jeff Anderson and Mike Maddox (Lion Hudson, 2000)

Oriel's Dairy, Robert Harrison (SU, 2002)

The Tale of Three Trees, Angela Elwell Hunt (Lion Hudson, 2009)

Make and Do Bible Crafts, Gillian Chapman and Leena Lane (Barnabas, 2009)

The Lion Easter Book, Mary Batchelor (Lion Hudson, 1989)

Literacy Trios, Easter, www.hopscotchbooks.com

The Spring Activity Book, Susan Vesey (Lion Hudson, 1987)

Ten-Minute Miracle Plays for Easter, Margaret Cooling (Bible Society, 2000); also *Ten-Minute Miracle Plays* covering the nativity, creation, Noah and Jesus in the temple

Assemblies from the Gallery, Margaret Cooling (RMEP, 2006) (now reissued with CD)

Jesus through Art, Margaret Cooling (RMEP, 1998)

Christmas Jokes, Puzzles and Poems, Sandy Ransford and Paul Cookson (Macmillan, 2001)

The Big Book of Christmas: poems, plays, carols and things to make and do, Gaby Morgan (Macmillan, 2005)

Multi-Sensory Seasons, Wendy Rayner and Annie Slade (SU, 2005)

Multi-Sensory Prayer, Sue Wallace (SU, 2000)

Multi-Sensory Church, Sue Wallace (SU, 2002)

All Together Now: 40 ready-to-use outlines for all-age worship, Christine Wright (SU, 2000)

It's Your Move, Nick Harding (SU, 2006)

The Works 2: poems on every subject and for every occasion, Brian Moses and Pie Corbett (Macmillan, 2002)

The Works 3: a poet for every week of the year, Paul Cookson (Macmillan, 2004)

Read Me: A Poem a Day for the National Year of Reading, Gaby Morgan (Macmillan, 1998)

Read Me Out Loud, Nick Toczek and Paul Cookson (Macmillan, 2007)

The Day I Fell Down the Toilet and Other Poems, Steve Turner (Lion Hudson, 1997)

The Easter Story Keepers, video and DVD
The Christmas Story Keepers, video and DVD
Miracle Maker DVD

The Lion, the Witch and the Wardrobe, C.S. Lewis (also available as a DVD)

The Pilgrim's Progress, John Bunyan

The Selfish Giant, Oscar Wilde

CD and booklet series called *Listen to This, Key Stage 1* (and its companion volume for KS2), which takes you on a grand tour of music from different historical periods and parts of the world. It is published by Saydisc Records (email: Saydisc@aol.com) and distributed by Music Education Supplies (email: music.mes@btconnect.com)

Poster sets available from McCrimmons Publishing (address below):
- Jesus, Our Way (12) £35
- Bread Broken (20) £52 or individually from about £6
- The Footsteps of Christ (16) £46
- Way of the Cross, posters of sculptures (14) £23

Websites and contact addresses

BRF (Bible Reading Fellowship)
15 The Chambers
Vineyard
Abingdon, OX14 3FE
United Kingdom
Tel: 01865 319700
Fax: 01865 319701
www.brf.org.uk
www.barnabasinschools.org.uk

Christian Aid
PO Box 100
London
SE1 7RT
www.christianaid.org.uk
Tel: 020 7620 4444

Tearfund
100 Church Road
Teddington
TW11 8QE
www.tearfund.org
Tel: 0845 355 8355

CAFOD
Romero Close
Stockwell Road
London
SW9 9TY
www.cafod.org.uk
Tel: 020 7733 7900
Fax: 020 7274 9630

Oxfam
Oxfam House
John Smith Drive
Cowley
Oxford
OX4 2JY
www.oxfam.org.uk
Tel: 0300 200 1300/01865 472602

Send a Cow
The Old Estate Yard
Newton St Loe
Bath
BA2 9BR
www.sendacow.org.uk
General enquiries: 01225 874 222